Now That I'm Here, What Should I Be Doing?

Discover Life's Purpose

Bill Harley & Jean Harley

Wisdom
Editions

Minneapolis, Minnesota

Wisdom
Editions
Minneapolis

FIRST EDITION MAY 2016
NOW THAT I'M HERE, WHAT SHOULD I BE DOING?
Copyright © 2016 by William B. Harley and Jean K. Harley.
All rights reserved.

Printed in the United States of America.
10 9 8 7 6 5 4 3 2 1

Cover and interior design: Gary Lindberg

ISBN: 978-1-939548-48-1

For Erin and Laura, Rich and Teddy, Sofia, Daniel and Kira

Contents

Acknowledgements

We wish to acknowledge the encouragement, insights and support of our many friends, associates and clients over numerous years as we worked on this book. In particular we wish to thank Marie Scheffer, Kimberly Kleis, Judy Milston, Martha Schweitz and Elizabeth Williams who either read the manuscript and gave us valuable feedback or encouraged us in other ways that made a major difference. In addition, we want to thank our publisher, Gary Lindberg, who read our large tome of a book and helped us see that two separate books needed to be extracted from the one.

Most of all, we want to thank our daughters, Erin Harley and Laura Harley, who championed this work, repeatedly read and critiqued evolving manuscripts, and never lost faith in our ability to finish it. Finally, we want to thank each other for unwavering, reciprocal support, patience, love, encouragement and effort without which this book would not have been completed.

"Then he came to a garden wall, and with untold pain he scaled it, for it proved very high; and forgetting his life, he threw himself down to the garden."

Bahá'u'lláh, *The Seven Valleys*, p. 13

Now That I'm Here, What Should I Be Doing?

Discover Life's Purpose

Bill Harley & Jean Harley

Chapter 1

The Search for Purpose

Our personal lives and professional experiences (as a life coach and a psychotherapist) have motivated us over several decades to search for the ultimate purposes of life in order to guide others and ourselves to greater meaning. The fruit of our search is this book about the purposes of life, the spiritual growth patterns designed into life, and how to make use of these purposes and patterns to live an optimally meaningful life.

From time immemorial human beings have wondered why they were born. Is there something we're supposed to be doing—or do we just survive and try to have some fun? A song written by Americans Jerry Leiber and Mike Stoller, and popularized by singer Peggy Lee in the 1960s and 70s, has relevant lyrics. After enumerating dramatic and emotional high and low points in life that seem without purpose and meaning, the song's closing lyrics are as follows:

Is that all there is, is that all there is?
If that's all there is my friends, then let's keep dancing.
Let's break out the booze and have a ball
If that's all there is.

For most of us, the song's central question is profound, but its answer is unsatisfactory. Somehow it seems that an All-Knowing,

All-Loving God would have more in mind for His creatures in terms of purpose. But what could that be?

Theologian Pierre Teilhard de Chardin is often credited with the statement "We are not human beings having a spiritual experience; we are spiritual beings having a human experience." However, the larger part of our lives seems to involve material experiences that are very human in nature. So, what does it mean to be a spiritual being, and how can we bring forth this dimension in our lives?

The Holy Writings of all the major religions, the repositories of guidance about the meaning and purposes of life, give clues that can be pieced together to provide answers and, sometimes, more questions. The Zoroastrian teachings say: "O pious one, you must purify the character!"[1] The Muslim teachings indicate that we need to look both outwardly and inwardly to discover God's purpose for us: "And of His signs is the creation of the heavens and the earth and the variety of your tongues and hues, surely there are signs in this for people who have knowledge."[2]

The Jewish teachings have us turn to our hearts to discover the mystery of our being: "As a man thinks in his heart, so is he."[3] The Hindu teachings also tell us to go inside to find a secret place that might reveal what we are to be doing: "In the city of Brahman is a secret dwelling, the lotus of the heart… As great as the infinite space beyond is the space within the lotus of the heart."[4] How do we purify our character, look around to discover God's signs, and think from our heart?

In the Christian teachings we are told: "You, therefore, must be perfect, as your heavenly Father is perfect."[5] This is an extraordinarily challenging purpose for us humans who usually prove to be anything but perfect. Further, the Christian teachings tell us: "Do you not know that you are God's temple and that God's spirit dwells in you?... For God's temple is holy, and that temple you are."[6] How do we go about our daily lives being "God's temple?" How do we manage the messy business of living while following all these dimensions of purpose?

The teachings of the Bahá'í Faith tell us: "The Purpose of the one true God, exalted be His glory, in revealing Himself unto men is to lay bare those gems that lie hidden within the mine of their true and inmost selves." [7] The Holy Writings of all the major religions indicate that every one of us has gems within us. So, it would seem that at least part of our work as spiritual beings is to bring forth as many of these gems as we can—in essence, to mine and polish these gems. But with all our weaknesses, our issues, our problems, how do we do that? And, if we can get clear about the ultimate purposes of life, what are the growth patterns we need to identify and the processes we need to go through to fulfill these purposes in our own personal way?

Our mission in the pages that follow is to discover answers to these very important questions. To do so, we will be exploring sacred scriptures from the world's revealed religions, and drawing upon our professional experiences coaching and counseling individuals and groups.

We will also be exploring, in-depth, a powerful parable that describes the spiritual growth patterns that have been designed into our lives by an all-loving Creator. Indeed, much of this book is devoted to examining the spiritual truths in this parable and how we can apply them in our own lives. We have found that when people go on this journey with us they discover aspects of themselves and their struggles that bring profound new insights to their lives. We will introduce this parable in Chapter 3; but for now, let us enter the path of discovery together.

Chapter 2

The Three Ultimate Purposes of Life

We have posed the question, *Now that I am here, what should I be doing?* In doing so, we are really considering human existence from a transcendent perspective and asking ourselves *what is the purpose of life on this earthly plane?*

A thorough review of the Holy Books of the world's major revealed religions [1] yields three ultimate and interrelated purposes of life: to know and love God, to develop spiritual attributes, and to carry forward an ever-advancing civilization. Let us consider each of these three purposes.

Life Purpose #1: To Know and Love God

In the Old Testament, Moses says to His followers:

> And thou shalt love the Lord thy God with all thine heart, and with all thy soul, and with all thy might. [2]

In the New Testament, Jesus Christ confirms Moses' teaching when He says:

> Thou shalt love the Lord thy God with all thy heart, and with all thy soul, and with all thy mind. This is the first and great commandment. [3]

A revealed prayer in the Bahá'í Scriptures states:

> I bear witness, O my God, that Thou hast created
> me to know Thee and to worship Thee. [4]

The life purpose of knowing, loving, and worshiping our Creator is a consistent theme throughout the centuries in the world's Holy Books. This suggests that life in the physical world should be used as a vehicle to strengthen our ability to know, become attracted to, and love our Creator. As we do so, we also develop our innate spiritual and intellectual capacities.

Life Purpose #2: To Develop Spiritual Attributes

The sacred texts of the world's religions are the repositories of the spiritual attributes we strive to develop in our earthly existence. As the foundation for her book, *The Family Virtues Guide*, Linda Kavelin Popov and her colleagues in The Virtues Project researched these sacred texts and found over three hundred key virtues or attributes propounded in common in these diverse faith traditions. [5] The centrality of spiritual virtues and attributes in these sacred texts makes it clear that their acquisition is a key purpose of our earthly existence. These are "the gems that lie hidden within the mine" of our "true and inmost selves" referred to earlier. We must mine and polish these virtues or attributes that lay latent within us and require a conscious effort to be brought forth and put into practice.

The focus placed by these sacred texts on the importance of developing spiritual attributes—such as forbearance, courtesy, mercy, purity, compassion, detachment, loving kindness, and a sense of justice—suggests that we are spiritual beings who are born into a physical body in order to have a human experience. Another way to look at this is that the spirit begins its eternal journey with a human experience, but continues this journey beyond this earthly plane into the spiritual realm where spiritual attributes will be essential.

A comparison can help us understand the importance of this work. [6] In the same way that a living human fetus is content in the confined realm of the mother's womb, yet must develop physical attributes such as eyes, ears, arms, and legs in order to be prepared to navigate the more spacious physical world it is moving toward, so living, breathing human beings may be content in this more spacious realm of the world. Yet they must develop spiritual attributes here such as courage, patience, generosity, selflessness, knowledge, honesty, and humility in order to be prepared to navigate the still more spacious spiritual world they are moving toward after this earthly existence. Just as failure to develop physical attributes while in the womb would handicap our earthly existence, failure to develop spiritual attributes while in this world would handicap our existence in the next world. Consequently, one of our purposes in this world is to persistently attend to our work of spiritual attribute development.

Life Purpose #3: To Carry Forward an Ever-Advancing Civilization

While Life Purposes #1 and #2 could conceivably justify people's focus solely on *self*-transformation, salvation, and the importance of the *next* world, Life Purpose #3 relates to *collective* transformation and salvation and the importance of society in *this* world. Concern for the welfare and progression of society is expressed in the world's Holy Writings as being in the hands of both God and those who are righteous.

The Holy Writings of Judaism convey the sense that the well-being of human society is dependent on spirituality and moral, ethical behavior.

> There are [always] thirty righteous men among nations, by whose virtue the nations of the world continue to exist. [7]

These same Writings also impart the idea that a spiritual connection to the Creator must be maintained to protect society.

> Except the Lord keep the city, the watchman wakes but in vain. [8]

In the Hindu Writings, we find the following:

> Strive constantly to serve the welfare of the world;
> by devotion to selfless work one attains the su-
> preme goal of life. Do your work with the welfare
> of others always in mind... The ignorant work for
> their own profit, Arjuna; the wise work for the wel-
> fare of the world, without thought to themselves. [9]

In the Holy Writings of Christianity, we find Jesus Christ's parable of the Good Samaritan, which tells the story of a man traveling along the road from Jerusalem to Jericho. He is beaten, robbed, and left for dead by the side of the road. A priest sees the helpless man lying by the roadside but passes him by on the other side of the road. Then a Levite does the same thing. The scripture continues:

> But a certain Samaritan as he journeyed, came
> where he was; and when he saw him, he had com-
> passion on him. And went to him, and bound up his
> wounds, pouring in oil and wine, and set him on
> his own beast, and brought him to an inn, and took
> care of him. [10]

While this noble story is usually taken to mean simply that we should be compassionate and nurturing to others, it can also be seen as a call to view all human beings as neighbors within one community and to progressively engage the larger society in effectively attending to the needs of all its members. After all, before leaving, the Samaritan takes an additional step.

> And on the next day, when he departed, he took
> out two denarii and gave them to the host, and said
> to him, Take care of him; and whatever thou spend-
> est more, when I come again, I will repay thee. [11]

The Samaritan makes provision for engaging *others* in delivering on-going care for the dispossessed. He advances the social compact.

In the Holy Writings of Islam we find these confirming words:

The best of men are those who are useful to others. [12]

In the Bahá'í Faith's Holy Writings, we find even more explicit exhortations in this regard.

All men have been created to carry forward an ever-advancing civilization. [13]

And:

Be anxiously concerned with the needs of the age ye live in, and center your deliberations on its exigencies and requirements. [14]

And:

Great is the station of man. Great must also be his endeavors for the rehabilitation of the world and the well-being of nations. [15]

Consequently, it is our mandate to build a civilization in which spiritual advancement guides and informs scientific, social, and technological advancement; a civilization in which individual and collective action are based on spiritual principles and values; and a civilization founded on service to others and having a concern for how one's thoughts, attitudes, communication, and actions contribute to the advancement or regression of human civilization.

Ultimately, this life purpose entails the responsibility of contributing to spiritual, scientific, and social advancement in the components of civilization—in the self, marriage, family, community, organization, city, state, nation, and global society at large. It involves having a concern for building justice, spirituality, compassion, unity, integrity, harmony, knowledge, civility, and coherence into civilization. In our daily lives, this might involve raising our children to be stronger than we are in spirituality, knowledge, and social conscience; or it could entail making honesty, integrity, and justice inform all of our acts both personally and professionally—even when it may work to our disadvantage materially.

Seen overall, fulfilling the first two purposes of life—knowing and loving God and developing spiritual attributes—helps us to achieve our individual, spiritual, and intellectual potential while bringing a spiritual orientation and spiritual attributes to fulfill the third purpose; and the third purpose—carrying forward an ever-advancing civilization—provides a social milieu and collective proving ground in which to practice and further develop all three purposes.

Chapter 3

The Dynamics of Growth on the Personal Path to Purpose

In Chapter 1, we posed questions about the ultimate purposes of life and then answered them in Chapter 2 based on a survey of the world's Holy Writings. At the end of Chapter 1, we also asked, "And, if we can get clear about the ultimate purposes of life, what are the growth patterns we need to identify and the processes we need to go through to fulfill these purposes in our own personal way?" This latter question is about the dynamics of change and spiritual growth each of us typically encounters on the way to achieving purposes, and we want to begin addressing it in this chapter.

Over the years, our own personal experiences with navigating change and spiritual growth, as well as our observations of our clients' experiences, have taught us that the pathway is more often winding than straight, the process more often messy than tidy, and the emotion more often disequilibrium than equilibrium. We noticed that there were many theoretical models of change and growth around, but we could find none that helped explain the role of our Creator in the process. We remained fascinated with the subject, but dissatisfied with our understanding.

Then, one day, we encountered a profound parable that helped us understand and begin honoring some of the dynamics of change and spiritual growth that are designed into life by an all-loving Creator. We refer to this parable as the "Watchman Parable," and it tells the story of a lover who is lost in hopeless suffering as a result of his seemingly unsuccessful search for his beloved.

Here is the parable:

> There was once a lover who had sighed for long years in separation from his beloved, and wasted in the fire of remoteness. From the rule of love, his heart was empty of patience, and his body weary of his spirit; he reckoned life without her as a mockery, and time consumed him away. How many a day he found no rest in longing for her; how many a night the pain of her kept him from sleep; his body was worn to a sigh, his heart's wound had turned him to a cry of sorrow. He had given a thousand lives for one taste of the cup of her presence, but it availed him not. The doctors knew no cure for him, and companions avoided his company; yea, physicians have no medicine for one sick of love, unless the favor of the beloved one deliver him.
>
> At last, the tree of his longing yielded the fruit of despair, and the fire of his hope fell to ashes. Then one night he could live no more, and he went out of his house and made for the marketplace. On a sudden, a watchman followed after him. He broke into a run, with the watchman following; then other watchmen came together, and barred every passage to the weary one. And the wretched one cried from his heart, and ran here and there, and moaned to himself: "Surely this watchman is 'Izra'il, my angel of death, following so fast upon me; or he is a tyrant of men, seeking to harm me." His feet carried him on, the one bleeding with the ar-

row of love, and his heart lamented. Then he came
to a garden wall, and with untold pain he scaled it,
for it proved very high; and forgetting his life, he
threw himself down to the garden.

And there he beheld his beloved with a lamp in
her hand, searching for a ring she had lost. When
the heart-surrendered lover looked on his ravishing love, he drew a great breath and raised up his
hands in prayer, crying: "O God! Give Thou glory
to the watchman, and riches and long life. For the
watchman was Gabriel, guiding this poor one; or
he was Israfil, bringing life to this wretched one!"

Indeed, his words were true, for he had found
many a secret justice in this seeming tyranny of
the watchman, and seen how many a mercy lay hid
behind the veil. Out of wrath, the guard had led
him who was athirst in love's desert to the sea of
his loved one, and lit up the dark night of absence
with the light of reunion. He had driven one who
was afar, into the garden of nearness, had guided
an ailing soul to the heart's physician.

Now if the lover could have looked ahead, he would
have blessed the watchman at the start, and prayed
on his behalf, and he would have seen that tyranny as justice; but since the end was veiled to him,
he moaned and made his plaint in the beginning.
Yet those who journey in the garden-land of knowledge, because they see the end in the beginning,
see peace in war and friendliness in anger.[1]

The Watchman Parable comes from a book called the *The Seven
Valleys* by Bahá'u'lláh,[2] the Prophet-Founder of the Bahá'í Faith.
The parable is based on the legendary story of the lovers, Layla and
Majnun, originating in ancient Arabia; however, Bahá'u'lláh has re-

fashioned the story to give it universal meaning in the context of the soul's journey through this world to its Creator.

Sensing that this parable carried a profound message, we read and reread it in order to better understand its significance; and we took the traditional stance that parables have universal application, that characters in them represent every man and every woman. The first thing that struck us was that the Watchman Parable described a process that, in the beginning, seemed accidental and damaging to the lover but in the end was personally tailored to produce growth in him. Considering the dynamics between the lover, the watchmen, the beloved, and the Creator in the parable, we asked ourselves, *could it be that life has been designed for each person as a personal learning and spiritual growth lab?* We turned to other Holy Books to see whether we could confirm this hypothesis.

The Learning & Spiritual Growth Lab of Life

In the Hindu Holy Writings, we find a description of this learning and spiritual growth lab.

> The policy of conquerors, the potency of kings,
> The great unbroken silence in learning's secret things;
> The lore of all the learned, the seed of all which springs.
> Living or lifeless, still or stirred, whatever beings be,
> None of them is in all the worlds, but it exists by Me! [3]

In the Christian Holy Writings, we find these words:

> For what can be known about God is plain to [all] because God has showed it to them. Ever since the creation of the world his invisible nature, namely, his eternal power and deity, has been clearly per-

ceived in the things that have been made. So they are without excuse. [4]

In the Holy Writings of Islam we read:

How many a sign there is in the heavens and the earth which most men pass by and ignore. [5]

And returning once again to the Holy Writings of the Bahá'í Faith, we find another description of the learning and spiritual growth lab of life.

I…have ordained for thy training every atom in existence and the essence of all things. [6]

Confirmed by both the Watchman Parable and the other scriptural references, we concluded that a compassionate Creator has designed a spiritual growth lab curriculum for each one of us tailored to the unique needs of our own mind, heart, and spirit. Just as in the parable, the intent of this curriculum is to give each of us repeated opportunities to make choices that will fulfill our spiritual potential and the ultimate purposes of life.

Further reflection about the Watchman Parable and the dynamics between the lover, the watchmen, the beloved, and the Creator led us to ask the additional question, *is it possible that a primary feature of the tailored learning and spiritual growth lab God has provided to each of us is the prevalence of tests and difficulties that are meant to provide us with opportunities for spiritual growth?* We turned to other Holy Books, to see whether we could confirm this hypothesis.

The Prevalence of Tests & Difficulties

In the Hindu Holy Writings, we find reference to the prevalence of suffering in life.

That which is beyond this world is without form and without suffering. They who know it, become immortal, but others suffer pain indeed. [7]

In the Buddhist Holy Writings, we find reference to the same.

> What, now, is the Noble Truth of Suffering? Birth is suffering; Decay is suffering; Death is suffering;
>
> Sorrow, Lamentation, Pain, Grief, and Despair, are suffering; not to get what one desires, is suffering; in short: the Five Groups of Existence are suffering. [8]

In the Christian Holy Writings, we find insight into the prevalence and purpose of suffering.

> Forasmuch then as Christ hath suffered for us in the flesh, arm yourselves likewise with the same mind: for he that hath suffered in the flesh hath ceased from sin; That he no longer should live the rest of his time in the flesh to the lusts of men, but to the will of God. [9]

In the Jewish Holy Writings, we see that suffering can come as a consequence of being off the path toward the three ultimate purposes of life.

> Slothfulness casteth into a deep sleep; and an idle soul shall suffer hunger. [10]

In the Muslim Holy Writings, the connection between suffering and learning is emphasized.

> Whenever We sent a prophet to a town, We took up its people in suffering and adversity, in order that they might learn humility. [11]

In the Bahá'í Holy Writings, we find further clarification about the value of tests, difficulties, and suffering.

> Tests are benefits from God, for which we should thank Him. Grief and sorrow do not come to us by chance, they are sent to us by the Divine Mercy for

our own perfecting. While a man is happy he may
forget his God; but when grief comes and sorrows
overwhelm him, then will he remember his Father
who is in Heaven, and who is able to deliver him
from his humiliations. [12]

Confirmed by both the Watchman Parable and the other scriptural references, we concluded that spiritual growth is achieved
largely by navigating through tests and difficulties in the spiritual
growth lab of life. Like the experience of the lover in the parable,
each of our life journeys is a spiritual drama that will bring us into
encounters with obstacles and suffering that are intended to perfect
us. Whether the sources of our suffering seem to be accidental, the
result of our own doing, or the doing of others, it is how we respond
to these difficulties that will determine whether we grow from them
or sink under their weight.

Answer Progress Report

So far, we have two answers to the question, *now that I am here,
what should I be doing*? The *first answer* is to fulfill the three ultimate purposes of life—to know and love God, to acquire spiritual attributes, and to carry forward an ever-advancing civilization.
The *second answer* is about the perspective we need to hold and it
has two dimensions: as we work on our own personal approach to
achieving the three purposes, we need to see the world as a spiritual
growth lab that provides a curriculum tailored to our own mind,
heart, and spirit; and we need to expect this tailored curriculum to
be characterized by tests and difficulties that we must navigate to
achieve our purposes. These two answers represent the larger spiritual drama of each of our lives.

Becoming Mindful of Our Own Spiritual Condition

The spiritual growth lab of life encourages us to become mindful
of the reality of our own spiritual condition from moment to moment. This reality is implicit in the two answers identified in the last

paragraph. In this book, we are defining the *reality of our spiritual condition* at any given moment as *the degree to which we (individually or collectively) are mindful of the value of tests in the spiritual growth lab of life and making progress on achieving the three purposes of life.*

Being mindful of our own spiritual condition in this way enables us to change our approach to life. Rather than passively flowing along with the currents of our culture and being preoccupied with the material "stuff" of life, we can proactively consider the spiritual implications behind the material conditions and our struggles with others. We can consider the spiritual implications of what we think and do and consider not just the "what" of things, but the "how" and "why." For example, if we are mindful of the three purposes of life and how they relate to each other, we can consider whether or not the way we intend to go about something will strengthen our connection with God, foster the development of our spiritual attributes, and serve our fellow human beings in a way that advances civilization. By changing our perspective in this way, we prepare ourselves to leverage the forces of both the spiritual growth lab of life and the tests and difficulties we encounter to make wiser choices that will fulfill our spiritual potential.

The Challenge of Keeping the Focus on Our Spiritual Condition

One of the challenges of manifesting the two answers in action is that the pull of the outer material world can keep us so busy that we can easily lose sight of the larger spiritual drama. The temporal or physical reality can blind us to the spiritual reality. When this happens, the noble part of ourselves that is equipped to see the big spiritual picture of our life, respond to divine guidance, and make wise decisions becomes overwhelmed; and then life's events can seem random and purposeless.

Yet, one of the Watchman Parable's messages seems to be that God sends the watchmen into our lives in succession to awaken the noble self in us. In other words, the dynamics of change and spiritual growth in our earthly existence have been designed by a compassionate Creator to continually provide tests as *reminders* to us of the larger spiritual reality in our life and *new opportunities* to make choices that can enable our noble self to refocus, reengage, and grow.

Further Exploring the Watchman Parable & the Spiritual Growth Lab of Life

Having established increased clarity about the purposes of life and the growth lab context in which we try to fulfill them, let us now return to the Watchman Parable to see what else it can teach us about the spiritual growth lab of life and the dynamics of change and spiritual growth each of us must manage in order to fulfill our potential.

Chapter 4

The Spiritual Growth Lab of Life Is Calling Us Toward Spiritual Reality

Examining the Watchman Parable and other scriptural references more closely can help us understand five apparent truths about the spiritual growth lab of life and what we should be doing during our time on earth. An understanding of these truths can help us effectively and expeditiously navigate the pathways to our beloveds. The first of these apparent truths is that *the spiritual growth lab of life is calling us toward spiritual reality.*

The Interplay between Material Reality & Spiritual Reality

The parable gives us insight into the interplay between material reality and spiritual reality. On one side of the wall, the lover's perspective is grounded in material reality. When the watchmen appear, he sees them two-dimensionally and assumes they are enemies locked with him in the physical struggle for survival. On the other side of the wall, his perspective becomes grounded in spiritual reality. He is able to see things three-dimensionally—in terms of his own role, the role of the watchmen, and that of his Creator. Through the grace of God and his own struggles, the lover learns: the two perspectives are radically different; the forces of both material and spiritual reality are constantly at play on both sides of the wall; and he has a choice over what perspective he will hold.

Becoming a Seeker of Spiritual Reality

The Watchman Parable suggests that we are designed to go through our earthly life in the spirit of a seeker grounded in spiritual reality. As discussed earlier, we seem to have a built-in longing for deeper meaning, clarity of purpose, and fulfillment during our brief time on earth; and the lover's search for a beloved can be seen to contain these longings. The parable conveys that on this seeking path we are designed to be mindful and reflective about our own role, the roles of others, and the role of our Creator as our hearts and souls prompt us to discover the truth.

Other Holy Writings also confirm the value of being a seeker of spiritual reality.

In the Judaic Writings, God says:

> Then shall ye call upon me, and ye shall go and pray unto me, and I will hearken unto you. And ye shall seek me, and find me, when ye shall search for me with all your heart.[1]

In the Christian Writings, Jesus Christ says:

> Ask, and it shall be given you; seek, and ye shall find; knock, and it shall be opened unto you: For every one that asketh receiveth; and he that seeketh findeth; and to him that knocketh it shall be opened.[2]

In terms of daily action, what does it mean for us to take these spiritual admonitions to heart? It would seem to involve discovering the unique gifts and capacities God has given us and then putting them to use in a way that is aligned with the three purposes of life.

The Potential Subversion of Our Search for Spiritual Reality

If our hearts and souls have been given a healthy spiritual education, they seek, by their very nature, to develop and manifest divine attributes such as compassion, generosity, joy, humility, faithfulness, fair-mindedness, understanding, detachment, helpfulness, patience, courtesy, acceptance, loving-kindness, curiosity, thoughtfulness, and a sense of justice. However, in materialistic cultures, spiritual potential can be subverted and energies diverted toward the acquisition of worldly attributes, material objects, and temporal power and influence. For example, the soul's inherent desire to acquire spiritual perfections is pushed aside by advertisers and other cultural forces seeking to provoke a desire for material or temporal things that will supposedly bring us fulfillment, respect, and attention. For example, a person who wins the lottery or acquires a luxury vehicle will be depicted by the media as having achieved ultimate joy and fulfillment. In addition, materialistic cultures teach us to look for quick, expedient fixes when we are feeling spiritually, physically, or emotionally uncomfortable, rather than going through the hard, but spiritually rewarding, work of seeking spiritual reality. For example, a feeling of spiritual emptiness might be addressed by consuming food, or using anesthetizing medicines or mind-altering drugs. Or a conflictual situation might be defined and addressed in adversarial terms leaving the parties angry and judgmental rather than enlightened by deeper awareness and understanding.

All of us absorb at least some of these cultural dictates that surround us. Some of what we learn from our families of origin, our schools, our other institutions and organizations, and our communities and cultures about what constitutes success and fulfillment is neither truth nor reality from a spiritual standpoint. *But the spiritual growth lab of life continues to call us toward spiritual reality.* Regardless of how much material wealth and worldly power we acquire, the spiritual longings of our hearts and souls are not stilled. The longings may be experienced as pangs of conscience, depression, a sense of emptiness, addictive behaviors, or a compulsive desire to acquire still more, accompanied by the nagging thought, "Is that all there is?" The spiritual growth lab of life summons us repeatedly to listen to and honor our spiritual longings. The lover in the parable is confronted by watchman after watchman until he awakens to spiritual reality.

Material Happiness Is Only Temporary Alleviation

The Holy Writings comment repeatedly about the relationship between material things and spiritual things. Guidance from Judaism says:

> Man shall not live by bread alone, but by every word that proceeds from the mouth of God.[3]

Guidance from Buddhism conveys:

> The impulse "I want" and the impulse "I'll have"—lose them! That is where people get stuck; without those, you can use your eyes to guide you through this suffering state. [4]

In Christianity, we find additional perspective.

> No one can serve two masters; for either he will hate the one and love the other, or he will be devoted to the one and despise the other. You cannot serve God and mammon.[5]

In Islam, we gain further insight.

> When they see merchandise or diversion they scatter off to it, and they leave you standing. Say, "What is with God is better than diversion and merchandise. God is the best of providers."[6]

The problem with material acquisitions and remedies is that they provide only brief, temporary relief from our deeper longings and the rigors of life. Beverages can alleviate thirst, food can alleviate hunger, a big house or a professional title may make us feel powerful, plastic surgery may make us feel more attractive—but all only for a very limited span of time. Alleviations are not joys in themselves. The Bahá'í Writings say:

> When a man is thirsty he drinks water. When he is hungry he eats food. But if a man be not thirsty,

water gives him no pleasure and if his hunger be already satisfied, food is distasteful to him.

This is not so with spiritual enjoyments. Spiritual enjoyments bring always joy. The love of God brings endless happiness. These are joys in themselves and not alleviations....Consider the nature of material happiness. It is something which but slightly removes one's afflictions; yet the people imagine it to be joy, delight, exultation and blessing. All the material blessings, including food, drink, etc., tend only to allay thirst, hunger, and fatigue. They bestow no delight on the mind nor pleasure on the soul...

As to spiritual happiness, this is the true basis of the life of man, for life is created for happiness, not for sorrow; for pleasure, not for grief. Happiness is life; sorrow is death. Spiritual happiness is life eternal. This is a light which is not followed by darkness. This is an honor which is not followed by shame... This great blessing and precious gift is obtained by man only through the guidance of God...[7]

Spiritual Oppression, the Watchman Parable, and Seeking Spiritual Reality

Living according to the conditioned learning we receive from our culture can lead to *spiritual oppression*, a state in which we cannot find an authentic source of spiritual sustenance. When this happens, we feel weighed down in body, mind, and spirit by the authority and influence the purely materialistic interpretation of life exercises over our spiritual being.

Spiritual oppression is characterized by depression, lack of energy, and even hopelessness. It undermines the drive to seek spiritual reality by sapping mental acuity and physical strength. This seems to be another lesson of the Watchman Parable. When the parable begins, the lover has struggled and suffered greatly in his longing for the beloved, but seems to have exhausted the conventional remedies propounded by his culture to enhance well-being. We are told that "the doctors knew no cure for him, and companions avoided his company." Neither medicine nor social interaction has provided him solace—his heart is still in pain. Consequently, he sinks into spiritual oppression—weighed down and growing hopeless from living his days without any authentic progress toward true peace, meaning, and fulfillment (the beloved).

But even in this increasingly hopeless state, the lover's longing cannot be stilled, and it calls him to forward movement. The intensification of his misery and the promptings of his heart make him go "out of his house" into uncomfortable and untried territory. He struggles both to find the beloved and a way out of his misery but is thwarted by the watchmen at every turn. His defensive and suspicious reactions to the watchmen reflect the limitations of his culturally-driven, materialistic world-view. Yet the lover struggles on and discovers that the dynamic forces God has built into the spiritual growth lab of life enable him to transcend his world view, scale the wall separating him from his beloved, and see his Creator, the watchmen, and the beloved with spiritual eyes. He moves from dependence on a purely material perspective to recognition of spiritual truth and reality. Ultimately, the lover recognizes the value of becoming a *wall-seeker* rather than a *wall-avoider* in order to use the spiritual growth lab of life optimally.

Becoming a Wall-Seeker

Continued reflection on the Watchman Parable and attempts to apply its lessons, led us to create the term "Wall-Seeker" and arrive at some preliminary definitions:

> **wall**, n **1**: an obstacle, impediment or boundary; **2**: a structure, force, or dynamic that separates one from objects or conditions existing on the other side.

seeker, n **1:** one who is in a state of active search, discovery, or inquiry; **2:** one searching for something more or different; **3:** one who strives to go beyond.

wall-seeker, n **1:** one who views walls as indicators of the existence of something precious waiting unseen, nearby; **2:** one who welcomes walls as mileposts to be scaled on the journey toward growth and greater spiritual awareness; **3:** one who views opposing or challenging forces as divine emissaries and guides; **4:** one who makes decisions and takes action accordingly.

So, Wall-Seekers are people who investigate reality by seeing with a spiritual eye and hearing with a spiritual ear. Their approach to the spiritual growth lab of life is embodied in the following passage from the Bahá'í Writings:

> God has given man the eye of investigation by which he may see and recognize truth. He has endowed man with ears that he may hear the message of reality and conferred upon him the gift of reason by which he may discover things for himself. This is his endowment and equipment for the investigation of reality. Man is not intended to see through the eyes of another, hear through another's ears nor comprehend with another's brain. Each human creature has individual endowment, power and responsibility in the creative plan of God. Therefore depend upon your own reason and judgment and adhere to the outcome of your own investigation; otherwise you will be utterly submerged in the sea of ignorance and deprived of all the bounties of God. Turn to God, supplicate humbly at His threshold, seeking assistance and confirmation, that God may rend asunder the veils that obscure your vision.[8]

As they navigate the spiritual growth lab of life and strive to achieve the three purposes of life, Wall-Seekers are also attentive to a number of additional principles drawn from the Watchman Parable that will be enumerated and further illustrated in this and the following chapters.

WALL-SEEKER PRINCIPLE:
Suffering & Loss Are Inherent in the Process
of Change & Spiritual Growth

The Watchman Parable is a story of suffering and loss leading to insight and the knowledge of spiritual reality. The lover experiences intense suffering and loss prior to going over the wall and gaining his heart's desire. Such words as "sighed," "separation," "wasted," "empty of patience," "weary," "consumed," "longing," "pain," "worn to a sigh," or "a cry of sorrow" convey the intensity of this suffering. The parable seems to suggest that our dissatisfaction with the present situation may need to increase to the level of real pain and suffering before we are moved to make a change. Further, the parable suggests that moving away from the limited nature of material reality toward a greater focus on spiritual reality will require that we navigate through tests and difficulties tailored specifically for our own growth needs. This is evident in the fact that the watchmen in the parable block the lover's path, but not the path of others.

The inseparability of spiritual growth from suffering, loss, tests, and difficulties is confirmed by other Holy Writings as well. In the Hindu Writings, spiritual knowledge and wisdom are seen as the product of suffering.

> **As the heat of the fire reduces wood to ashes, the fire of knowledge burns to ashes all karma. Nothing in this world purifies like spiritual wisdom.**[9]

The Judaic Writings also use the image of fire to suggest that suffering and tests can improve us.

> If a man draws near the fire, he derives benefit; if he keeps afar, he is frozen, so with the words of the Torah: if a man toils in them, they are life to him; if he separates from him, they kill him. [10]

In the Buddhist Writings, we find the idea that the tailored tests and sufferings sent our way by God will protect us from worse suffering.

> Yet the suffering
> Involved in my awakening will have limit;
> It is like the suffering of having an incision made
> In order to remove and destroy greater pain. [11]

In the Christian Writings, the contribution of suffering to spiritual growth is emphasized.

> Three times I [Paul] besought the Lord about this [suffering], that it should leave me; but he said to me, "My grace is sufficient for you, for my power is made perfect in weakness." I will all the more gladly boast of my weaknesses, that the power of Christ may rest upon me. For the sake of Christ, then, I am content with weaknesses, insult, hardships, persecutions, and calamities; for when I am weak, then I am strong. [12]

The Muslim Writings also emphasize the growth-producing value of trials and ordeals.

> Every soul must taste of death, and We try you with evil and with good, for ordeal. And unto Us you will be returned. [13]

And the Bahá'í Writings add further to our understanding.

The mind and spirit of man advance when he
is tried by suffering. The more the ground is
ploughed the better the seed will grow, the better the harvest will be. Just as the plough furrows
the earth deeply, purifying it of weeds and this-
tles, so suffering and tribulation free man from the
petty affairs of this worldly life until he arrives at a
state of complete detachment. His attitude in this
world will be that of divine happiness. Man is, so to
speak, unripe: the heat of the fire of suffering will
mature him. Look back to the times past and you
will find that the greatest men have suffered most.
Through suffering he will attain to an eternal happiness which nothing can take from him.[14]

So, like the lover in the Watchman Parable, we must be ripened
or matured by "the heat of the fire of suffering" in order to grow
spiritually and maintain a spiritual perspective. Struggle in this life
is the crucible that can forge spiritual attributes and progression.

WALL-SEEKER PRINCIPLE:
*There Is Joy Somewhere on the Other Side of
the Wall*

The preceding quotation conveys that "Through suffering" we
"will attain to an eternal happiness." The Watchman Parable, too,
suggests that for those willing to persevere through trials and scale
the walls in their lives, the joy of fulfillment is readily available.
Furthermore, the parable seems to convey that the joy of fulfillment
is designed into the very process of change and spiritual growth,
and that a compassionate God promises the joy of reunion to every
sincere seeker. Other Holy Writings also convey this principle. The
Hindu Writings suggest that the outcomes of goodness and virtue
tend to prevail in God's creation.

Ambrosia can be extracted even from poison; elegant speech even from a child; good conduct even from an enemy, gold even from impurity.[15]

The Judaic Writings describe this principle in terms of God's discipline.

My son, do not despise the Lord's discipline
or be weary of his reproof,
for the Lord reproves him who he loves,
as a father the son in whom he delights.[16]

And the Bahá'í Writings further emphasize that joy issues forth from perseverance on the path of spiritual truth.

Let not the happenings of the world sadden you. I swear by God! The sea of joy yearneth to attain your presence, for every good thing hath been created for you, and will, according to the needs of the times, be revealed unto you.[17]

Given our likely immersion in struggle and suffering as we navigate through the spiritual growth lab of life toward the joy of the beloved's presence, the Watchman Parable suggests another principle that can help us on our journeys.

WALL-SEEKER PRINCIPLE:
*The "Beloved" May Look Different and/or Be
in a Different Place than We Had Expected*

Two of the preceding quotes say respectively that to advance spiritually we need to supplicate God to "rend asunder the veils that obscure" our vision, and that tribulation will free us "from the petty affairs of this worldly life." Both of these references suggest that becoming more focused on spiritual reality requires a radical reorientation involving detachment from material reality and learning to see without intervening obstructions or presumptions.

Similarly, the Watchman Parable indicates that we may need to reorient our expectations and sharpen our vision as we strive to find and fulfill our purpose—because when we find the thing we seek (the beloved), it may look different or be in a different place than we had expected. There is great irony implicit in the scene where the lover, trying to escape the watchmen, throws himself off the top of the wall down into the darkness of the garden and discovers his beloved. Not only does she appear in a place where the lover had no expectation of finding her, but she too is searching in darkness. In addition, under normal circumstances, when one pictures the beloved, or the ultimate goal of a quest, it appears as a settled destination; but here the beloved appears *moving* through darkness, even as the lover has been moving through the dark night. As a compensation for the unexpected location and manner of her appearance, attention is called to her presence by the fact that she is walking "…with a lamp in her hand." The parable suggests to us that *the unexpected* is a central component of the spiritual growth process and *alertness* and *seeing with unobscured vision* will be required of the seeker.

Using the Womb of this World to Become Focused on Spiritual Reality

If the spiritual growth lab of life is calling us toward spiritual reality, why is it important that we respond to the call? The Holy Writings indicate that there are spiritual worlds beyond this material one to which our spirits will be moving. The Hindu Writings describe correspondences between this world and the next.

> What is here [the phenomenal world], the same is there [in Brahman]; and what is there, the same is here.[18]

The Christian Writings assure us of the great expanse of the spiritual worlds beyond this one.

In my Father's house are many rooms. [19]

The Writings of Islam make a similar assertion.

God created the seven heavens in harmony. [20]

The Bahá'í Writings exhort us to relax our grip on the material world and become mindful even now of our movement toward the next spiritual world.

> **Say: If ye be seekers after this life and the vanities thereof, ye should have sought them while ye were still enclosed in your mothers' wombs, for at that time ye were continually approaching them, could ye but perceive it. Ye have, on the other hand, ever since ye were born and attained maturity, been all the while receding from the world...** [21]

The image of the womb, as mentioned earlier, is instructive. The wombs of our mothers give way to the womb of this world, and the womb of this world gives way to spiritual worlds beyond. So, in the womb of this world, we need to be developing qualities that we will need to navigate the spiritual world beyond this one. The spiritual growth lab of life seems to be continually presenting us with tests and difficulties that, if handled according to the Holy Writings, will successfully prepare us for our role in the next world.

What do we know about the nature of the next world or heaven? In the Christian Writings, we get a glimpse of the difference between the nature of the material and spiritual worlds.

> **For we know in part, and we prophesy in part. But when that which is perfect is come, then that which is in part shall be done away. When I was a child, I spake as a child, I understood as a child, I thought as a child: but when I became a man, I put away childish things. For now we see through a glass, darkly; but then face to face: now I know in part; but then shall I know even as also I am known.** [22]

In the Bahá'í Writings, we get another glimpse.

> Therefore in this world he must prepare himself for the life beyond. That which he needs in the world of the Kingdom must be obtained here. Just as he prepared himself in the world of the matrix [womb] by acquiring forces necessary in this sphere of existence, so likewise the indispensable forces of the divine existence must be potentially attained in this world.
>
> What is he in need of in the Kingdom which transcends the life and limitation of this mortal sphere? That world beyond is a world of sanctity and radiance; therefore it is necessary that in this world he should acquire these divine attributes. In that world there is need of spirituality, faith, assurance, the knowledge and love of God. These he must attain in this world so that after his ascension from the earthly to the heavenly Kingdom he shall find all that is needful in that life eternal ready for him.
>
> That divine world is manifestly a world of lights; therefore man has need of illumination here. That is a world of love; the love of God is essential. It is a world of perfections; virtues or perfections must be acquired. That world is vivified by the breaths of the Holy Spirit; in this world we must seek them. That is the Kingdom of life everlasting; it must be attained during this vanishing existence.[23]

Using the Science of Reality Revealed by the Divine Messengers

How can we reframe our vision in order to see through a lens that expedites the investigation of spiritual reality and the successful movement toward the spiritual world beyond this one? The Holy Writings indicate that the purpose of the divine Messengers Who founded the world's major revealed religions is to provide this lens. God has sent these Figures to progressively serve as our educators and guides for this transformative process. Their examples, laws, and teachings provide the remedies for our ignorance. For example, the Hindu Writings say:

> Those who live in accordance with the divine laws without complaining, firmly established in faith, are released from karma. Those who violate these laws, criticizing and complaining, are utterly deluded, and are the cause of their own suffering. [24]

The Judaic Writings use a simile to explain this concept.

> Blessed is the man
> Who walks not in the counsel of the wicked,
> Nor sits in the seat of scoffers;
> but his delight is in the law of the Lord, and on His law he meditates day and night.
> He is like a tree
> planted by streams of water,
> that yields its fruit in its season
> and its leaf does not wither.
> In all that he does, he prospers. [25]

The Muslim Writings also use the image of a tree.

> A good word is as a good tree—
> its roots are firm,
> and its branches are in heaven;
> its gives its produce every season
> by the leave of its Lord.
> So God strikes similitudes for men;
> haply they will remember.

And the likeness of a corrupt word
is as a corrupt tree—
uprooted from the earth,
having no establishment.
God confirms those who believe with the firm word,
in the present life and in the world to come;
and God leads astray the evildoers;
and God does what He will. [26]

In the Christian Writings, a different image is used.

Every one then who hears these words of mine
and does them will be like a wise man who built
his house upon the rock; and the rain fell, and the
floods came, and the winds blew and beat upon
that house, but it did not fall, because it had been
founded on the rock. And every one who hears
these words of mine and does not do them will be
like a foolish man who built his house upon the
sand; and the rain fell, and the floods came, and
the winds blew and beat against that house, and it
fell; and great was the fall of it. [27]

And in the Bahá'í Writings, we find additional insights about
these divine Educators.

It is evident therefore that man is in need of divine
education and inspiration; that the spirit and boun-
ties of God are essential to his development. That is
to say, the teachings of Christ and the Prophets are
necessary for his education and guidance. Why?
Because they are the divine gardeners who till the
earth of human hearts and minds. They educate
man, uproot the weeds, burn the thorns and re-
model the waste places into gardens and orchards
where fruitful trees grow. The wisdom and purpose

of their training is that man must pass from degree to degree of progressive unfoldment until perfection is attained.[28]

And:

The Prophets of God have been the servants of reality; Their teachings constitute the science of reality.[29]

Being Called to Spiritual Reality

In summary, to be called to spiritual reality by the spiritual growth lab of life is: to be called to fulfilling the three purposes of life; to be called to the path of the true seeker *and* to that of the Wall-Seeker; to be called to the experience of tests, difficulties, and suffering as a medium of spiritual growth and to the experience of joy on the other side of the wall; to be called to expect the unexpected in the search for the beloved; to be called to use the womb provided by this material world to build spiritual capacity for the next; and to use the science of reality revealed by the divine Messengers.

Chapter 5

The Spiritual Growth Lab of Life Is Calling Forth Our True Self

The second of the five truths that the Watchman Parable seems to teach us, in order to better use our time on earth, is that *the spiritual growth lab of life is calling forth our true self.*

Knowing One's Self

If this is so, it suggests that a key desired outcome from one's earthly existence is to know one's self. Other Holy Writings also confirm this desired outcome. The Hindu Writings tell us:

> Man should discover his own reality
> and not thwart himself.
> For he has his self as his only friend,
> or as his only enemy.
>
> A person has the self as friend
> when he has conquered himself,
> but if he rejects his own reality,
> the self will war against him. [1]

In the Writings of Judaism we read:

> If I am not for myself who is for me? And when I am for myself what am I? And if not now, when? [2]

In the Buddhist Writings we find:

> Not by travelling to the end of the world can one accomplish the end of ill. It is in this fathom-long carcass, friend, with its impressions and its ideas that, I declare, lies the world, and the cause of the world, and the cessation of the world, and the course of action that leads to the cessation of the world. [3]

The Christian Writings say:

> Work out your own salvation with fear and trembling. [4]

The Muslim Writings add:

> O ye who believe! You have charge over your own souls. [5]

In the Writings of the Bahá'í Faith we read:

> ...the first effulgence which hath dawned from the horizon of the Mother Book is that man should know his own self and recognize that which leadeth unto loftiness or lowliness, glory or abasement, wealth or poverty. [6]

The lover's experiences in the Watchman Parable help him to learn about the larger spiritual reality, about his own self, and about what leads to its "loftiness or lowliness, glory or abasement, wealth or poverty."

The True Self & the World's Religious Scriptures

The noble or true self, which resides in each of us, is a major theme in the Holy Writings of the world's major religions. Here is a small

sampling from some of these sacred texts from the most ancient to
the most recent:

Bright but hidden, the Self dwells in the heart.
Everything that moves, breathes, opens, and closes
Lives in the Self. He is the source of love
And may be known through love but not
Through thought.
He is the goal of life. Attain this goal! [7]

Hinduism

God said, "Let us make man in our image, after our
likeness." [8]

Judaism

Let a man always consider himself as if the Holy
One dwells within him. [9]

Judaism

Every being has the Buddha Nature. This is the
self. [10]

Buddhism

I am in my Father, and you in me, and I in you. [11]

Christianity

Do you not know that you are God's temple and
that God's Spirit dwells in you?... For God's temple
is holy, and that temple you are. [12]

Christianity

I have breathed into man of My spirit. [13]

Islam

Thou art My lamp and My light is in thee. [14]

Bahá'í Faith

This noble "self" is our soul or spiritual essence, which has the capacity to stay connected to the world of the spirit. Made in the image of God, our noble self has the attributes of God latent within it. Spiritual growth and development, then, involves persistently working to develop and express these attributes in daily life. George Townshend, religious scholar and author, says:

> The divine image in man is part of himself, it is indeed his true self, the essence of his existence, the soul of his soul. In purifying his heart that this likeness may shine forth in its beauty and in its truth, he is not only drawing near to God but is also becoming himself, is finding himself: he passes out of spiritual weakness and infancy into maturity. His faculties and endowments, aided by the law of growth, establish among themselves a balance and symmetry and order; he is happy and wins that rest unto his soul which Christ promised to those who came to Him. If through neglect he does not cause the heavenly qualities within to expand, the loss is his. He stunts himself, he limits himself; he chooses infirmity instead of power. [15]

The True Self & the Other Self

In the Watchman Parable, the lover also discovers that one purpose of our experiences in the spiritual growth lab of life is to learn to manage the dualism described in a preceding quote between loftiness and lowliness, between glory or abasement—the tension in the human reality—in such a way that we increasingly reside in and act from our wisest and noblest self. Other Holy Writings echo this message. In the Judaic Writings, we find:

> And the Lord said to Moses, "Say to all the congregation of the people of Israel, 'You shall be holy; for I the Lord your God am holy.'" [16]

The Buddhist Writings say:

> By self do you censure self. By self do you examine yourself. Self-guarded and mindful, O bhikkhu, you will live happily.

> Self, indeed, is the protector of self. Self, indeed, is one's refuge. Control, therefore, your own self as a merchant controls a noble steed. [17]

The Muslim Writings add:

> Whoever works righteousness benefits his own soul; whoever works evil, it is against his own soul: Your Lord is never unjust to His servants. [18]

And the Bahá'í Writings impart the following:

> O MY SERVANT!
> Thou art even as a finely tempered sword concealed in the darkness of its sheath and its value hidden from the artificer's knowledge. Wherefore come forth from the sheath of self and desire that thy worth may be made resplendent and manifest unto all the world. [19]

So, while each of us has an inner or true self that is like "a finely tempered sword," it may be concealed in a sheath representing another self that is characterized by inner "darkness" and "desire." This dark and desire-laden self would seem to be our lower nature that is attached to the material world. On the other hand, the true self, represented by the sword, is our spiritual or higher nature which is characterized by light and radiance. When it comes forth out of the sheath, its "worth may be made resplendent."

Managing the Conflict Within

The Holy Writings challenge us to learn to manage the conflict within us. The Christian Writings give us insight into this struggle.

So I find it to be a law that when I want to do right, evil lies close at hand. For I delight in the law of God, in my inmost self, but I see in my members another law at war with the law of my mind and making me captive to the law of sin which dwells in my members. Wretched man that I am! Who will deliver me from this body of death? [20]

The Hindu Writings describe the dynamics of managing the inner conflict.

> I know what is good
> but I am not inclined to do it;
> I know also what is bad,
> but I do not refrain from doing it;
> I just do as I am prompted to do
> by some divine spirit
> standing in my heart. [21]

The Zoroastrian Writings describe the potential outcomes of managing this conflict.

> Yes, there are two fundamental spirits, twins which are renowned to be in conflict. In thought and in word, in action, they are two: the good and the bad. And between these two, the beneficent have correctly chosen, not the maleficent. [22]

Additional insight from the Hindu Writings suggests the key to managing the inner conflict.

> The mind is said to be twofold:
> The pure and also the impure;
> Impure—by union with desire;
> Pure—from desire completely free. [23]

And the Bahá'í Writings clarify even further the key to managing the inner conflict.

For the world of nature is an animal world. Until
man is born again from the world of nature—that is
to say, becomes detached from the world of nature,
he is essentially an animal, and it is the teachings of
God which convert this animal into a human soul.[24]

The "Inmost True Self" & the Manifestations of God

In order to nurture the human soul, the capacity for goodness and
nobility, the divine Messengers have addressed Their words and
teachings to each person's true self. Clarifying the purpose of the
missions of these divine Messengers, the Bahá'í Writings say:

> In the kingdoms of earth and heaven there must
> needs be manifested a Being, an Essence Who
> shall act as a Manifestation and Vehicle for the
> transmission of the grace of the Divinity Itself, the
> Sovereign Lord of all. Through the Teachings of
> this Day Star of Truth every man will advance and
> develop until he attaineth the station at which he
> can manifest all the potential forces with which his
> inmost true self hath been endowed. It is for this
> very purpose that in every age and dispensation
> the Prophets of God and His chosen Ones have ap-
> peared amongst men, and have evinced such pow-
> er as is born of God and such might as only the
> Eternal can reveal.[25]

It is clear that drawing forth the true self in each human being is
a primary purpose of these Messengers. If we think of the ministry
of Jesus Christ, for example, we can recall His ability to help "…
every man… advance and develop until he attaineth the station at
which he can manifest all the potential forces with which his inmost
true self hath been endowed." Like the other Messengers of God before and after Him, Jesus Christ addressed and called forth the true
self as witnessed by the Gospel of Mark in its description of Jesus
Christ's ability to recruit disciples.

Now after that John was put in prison, Jesus came into Galilee, preaching the gospel of the kingdom of God, and saying, the time is fulfilled, and the kingdom of God is at hand: repent ye, and believe the gospel.

Now as he walked by the sea of Galilee, he saw Simon and Andrew his brother casting a net into the sea: for they were fishers. And Jesus said unto them, Come ye after me, and I will make you to become fishers of men. And straightway they forsook their nets, and followed him.

And when he had gone a little farther thence, he saw James the son of Zebedee, and John his brother, who also were in the ship mending their nets. And straightway he called them: and they left their father Zebedee in the ship with the hired servants, and went after him. [26]

What aspect of Simon, Andrew, James, and John responded with such immediacy to the summons of Jesus Christ to let go of the lives they were leading and choose new lives of greater spiritual significance? It could only be the true self within each of them that resonated to the spiritual reality to which Jesus Christ was calling them.

The Aspiration & Capacity of the True Self

When this true self is connected to God and free from the world of nature and material attachments, its capacities are immense. The Hindu Writings attest:

> The shining Self dwells hidden in the heart.
> Everything in the cosmos, great and small,
> Lives in the Self. He is the source of life,
> Truth beyond the transience of this world.
> He is the goal of life. Attain this goal! [27]

If resonating and connected to its Creator, the true self also has exceptionally acute spiritual perception. The Author of the Watchman Parable describes in another place the qualities of the true seeker, which is also a description of the true self unencumbered by worldly attachments.

> I swear by God! Were he that treadeth the path of guidance and seeketh to scale the heights of righteousness to attain unto this glorious and exalted station, he would inhale, at a distance of a thousand leagues, the fragrance of God, and would perceive the resplendent morn of a Divine guidance rising above the Day Spring of all things. Each and every thing, however small, would be to him a revelation, leading him to his Beloved, the Object of his quest. So great shall be the discernment of this seeker that he will discriminate between truth and falsehood, even as he doth distinguish the sun from shadow. If in the uttermost corners of the East the sweet savors of God be wafted, he will assuredly recognize and inhale their fragrance, even though he be dwelling in the uttermost ends of the West. He will, likewise, clearly distinguish all the signs of God -- His wondrous utterances, His great works, and mighty deeds -- from the doings, the words and ways of men, even as the jeweler who knoweth the gem from the stone, or the man who distinguisheth the spring from autumn, and heat from cold. When the channel of the human soul is cleansed of all worldly and impeding attachments, it will unfailingly perceive the breath of the Beloved across immeasurable distances, and will, led by its perfume, attain and enter the City of Certitude.[28]

These capacities of the true self are essential because they make it possible for us to see with spiritual eyes as we navigate through the spiritual growth lab of life. This ability is also necessary if we are to make use of the following principle.

WALL-SEEKER PRINCIPLE:
Several Apparently Random, Unconnected Events in One's Life May Be Intensely Connected in Their Meaning to One's Life

---

The true self has tremendous capacity to deal with material reality while keeping a keen focus on spiritual reality. To better understand the spiritual acuity required to do this, we can compare the status of the lover's true self in the Watchman Parable before and after he goes over the wall.

When the lover leaves his home at the beginning of the parable, he is seeking the beloved and relief from his longing, pain, and suffering. Because he is preoccupied with material reality, he sees the watchmen as unrelated distractions drawing him away from his quest. They divert him away from his intended path by blocking his passage and ultimately driving him to a location to which he would not have arrived without their influence. In the mind of the lover, he has been driven entirely off course from his quest. Having sought relief from his suffering, his pain has now been increased, and he is fighting for his life against what he perceives to be the "angel of death." By all indications from his worldly perspective, he has lost ground in his quest and is failing.

However, from the larger spiritual perspective, these seemingly antagonistic or random forces have been sent from the divine realm and have put him exactly where he needs to be to achieve his quest. The watchmen have been key guiding instruments in bringing him to this point; and these apparently random, unconnected events and forces in his life are *intensely* connected in their *meaning* to his life. Before going over the wall, the lover, preoccupied with physical reality, is blind to this larger spiritual perspective because he is coming from fear and anguish rather than his true self; but after going over the wall, he can clearly see this larger spiritual reality because his true self has become fully engaged.

The parable suggests that these dynamics are relevant to all people's lives. When faced with the tests and difficulties inherent in life's spiritual growth lab, we often have a tendency to come from our *other self* rather than our *true self* and to experience the watchmen forces as disconnected and antagonistic. We may, for example, become angry and preoccupied with blaming the watchmen, thinking of ways to get even with them, or gossiping about their terrible qualities to others. However, if we can learn to come from our true self, the self that seeks to grow from our experiences, we can have the spiritual acuity to see that these forces, while apparently random, unconnected events in our life, are really intensely connected in their meaning to our life. The true self will keep us on track by working to understand what the watchmen forces (or obstacles) in our life are trying to teach us. For example, the forces could be trying to transform our greed into generosity, our prejudice into acceptance and appreciation, our anger into compassion, our hate into love. The true self has the capacity to acknowledge our weaknesses without defensiveness and commit to taking the steps to replace weaknesses with virtues.

Some Other Attributes of the True Self

When our true self is connected to the world of the spirit, we manifest authentic compassion, curiosity, and wisdom so that we are able to make healthy and holistic decisions. The spiritually-centered true self can effectively orchestrate the interplay of our spiritual and physical natures and guide us to stay on track, moving in the direction of the three ultimate purposes of life and our unique spiritual purposes as well. It is this self, which is inclined to seek and scale walls rather than avoid them, that does not despair in the face of obstacles and flee from discomfort, but sees such situations as tailored opportunities for growth.

Given the challenging cross-currents flowing through all of our lives from moment to moment, it can be difficult to know when our true self is in the lead and when it is not. The most reliable, quick-reference indicator that one is coming from the true self is that *one is able to feel compassion for one's self and for others simultaneously.* Applying this indicator to yourself means that feeling compassion for yourself while feeling harshly or coldly toward others indicates you are not coming from your true self; conversely, feeling compassion for others while feeling harshly or coldly toward yourself also indicates you are not coming from your true self. The true self is characterized by both incoming and outgoing compassion.

Compassion versus Pity

There is a distinction to be made between compassion and pity. While both terms imply sorrow for one in distress, pity is a relatively *passive* attribute which does not include the desire to alleviate suffering and may also include feeling condescension or even contempt toward the one suffering. Self-pity implies a victim rather than a learning mentality, a placing of responsibility on others rather than one's self, and a passive wallowing in sorrow for one's self without attempting to move forward and grow from it. Compassion, however, is an *active* attribute—it creates an energy—which moves one to mitigate the suffering of one's self or others through proactive and constructive means. It implies a greater attraction to, and sense of connection with, others than mere pity does. These distinctions help us to identify another principle from the parable.

WALL-SEEKER PRINCIPLE:
Having Both Self-Compassion & Compassion
for Others Deepens Understanding

In the Watchman Parable, the lover seems to be passive and lost in self-pity at the beginning of the story. However, there is evidence that he generates at least the beginning of self-compassion when, in the midst of his intense suffering, he arises in action and goes to the marketplace in an attempt to alleviate it. Nevertheless, the seedling of self-compassion, not yet fully formed, serves only to intensify the lover's suffering. He reacts to the watchmen in "fight or flight" mode with harsh feelings and defensiveness, running in one direction and then another without stopping to reflect. It never occurs to him that the watchmen may be beneficial guides, and he does not consider them in a thoughtful way. Rather, his interaction with them increases his own misery, prevents the deepening of his understanding, and lengthens his journey in search of the beloved.

But the spiritual growth lab of life relentlessly continues to operate on the lover until the watchmen corner him. Now the lover has no apparent path of escape, and the parable tells us that "his heart lamented." To lament is to express sorrow for, to mourn, and to bewail. Here, it appears, the self-compassion that had fueled the lover's movement into the marketplace comes into full bloom and is about to fuel his movement over the wall.

For the lover to experience self-compassion fully is for him to acknowledge and accept his own shortcomings, the poignancy of his own spiritual suffering, and his struggle toward the beloved and his Creator. *This is an important and counter-intuitive lesson that is part of the mystery of compassion.* It is at the moment when we are aware of our own short-comings, our own limitations, and our own dependence on the mercy and grace of God that we are in contact with self-compassion and with our true selves. When we embrace this place and acknowledge our presence there, the tendencies to blame, judge, criticize, and contend with others dissolve and our attention moves away from the watchmen in our lives to the wall we must scale. And this is exactly what happens to the lover—his eyes move away from the watchmen to the garden wall, and he begins to scale it. His true self is leading his being.

After going over the wall, the lover realizes that having both *self-compassion* for what he is going through and *compassion for others* with whom he is engaged are important for deepening understanding and accelerating spiritual growth. In the words of the parable:

When the heart-surrendered lover looked on his ravishing love, he drew a great breath and raised up his hands in prayer, crying: "O God! Give Thou glory to the watchman, and riches and long life. For the watchman was Gabriel, guiding this poor one."[29]

One would think that having finally found the object of his search, the lover would be totally pre-occupied with adoring the beloved. Instead, after first looking at her beauty and acknowledging her presence, the lover immediately expresses compassion for the watchmen when he beseeches God to bless and reward the watchmen for their efforts in guiding him to his beloved. The self-compassion in the lover's heart overflows into compassion for his previously perceived opponents. His true self is fully engaged.

The stark contrast between compassion and lack of compassion is well illustrated in the Watchman Parable. On the watchman side of the wall, the lover is alone in an antagonistic universe in which contending and compassionless parties locked into their own perspectives compete for survival. On the garden side of the wall, the lover is collaboratively connected to all other beings in a universe guided by a compassionate and loving God who cares for, and tends to, each person's spiritual progress in mystical and very personal ways. Once the lover goes over the wall into this new and compassionate world-view, his life experience dramatically changes.

Each of us must also choose one of these two world-views as we go through the spiritual growth lab of life. The true self in each of us chooses the second one. This allows us to realize that defensiveness (which can grow out of any number of feelings such as fear, anger, frustration, anxiety, shame, and panic) generates resistance to the change and spiritual growth processes God has designed into life and delays our progress toward the beloved. Rather than being defensive, the true self's incoming compassion attempts to alleviate inner suffering by asking questions that lead to understanding such as: What am I feeling? How can I make this situation better? What is not healthy for me in this situation? What do I need to do to remove myself from this toxic situation/relationship? What steps do I need to take toward spiritual growth?

The Challenge of Coming from the True Self

It is a huge challenge to consistently honor and come from one's true self while living this brief human experience. Yet this is the very thing the spiritual growth lab of life designed by our Creator is calling us to do. Part of the difficulty is that the material world, which is simply the vehicle through which we are to develop spiritual attributes, come to know and love God, and serve others in ways that advance civilization, can be so beguiling as to trap us into seeing it as the end rather than the means. When this happens, we begin to define success on the basis of public opinion and forget that we do not necessarily need power, position, titles, authority, and material wealth to achieve what we are here for.

There is nothing inherently wrong with having worldly things as long as we are primarily using them to better fulfill the three ultimate purposes of life. For example, using a position of authority to better serve all people with justice and honesty is commendable. However, power can corrupt. The trappings of worldly success can lead a person to forget that he or she is a spiritual being and to habitually function from the lower or material nature. When we invest our energies in developing our lower nature and connecting ourselves and our hearts to the material world, we are opposing not only the emergence of our true selves but the other forces of the spiritual growth lab of life as well. And because the deepest longings of our hearts are spiritual in nature, this opposition leads to frustration, disappointment, discouragement, emptiness, and hopelessness.

But despite all this, God stands continuously near, providing issues, opportunities, problems, and watchmen so that we will not lose our chance, will scale the walls before us, will learn to trust Him, engage in communion with Him, and achieve that imperishable glory that is the potential destiny of our true selves.

The Threat of Losing Our Chance

No matter what our past may have been, we can *choose* to turn toward God, set aside the limited standards of the world around us, and have our true selves lead our beings. The choice we are faced with is critical. Like the lover in the Watchman Parable, we can easily choose to contend with and run from the watchmen that show up in our lives whether they be difficult people, troubling situations, illnesses, loss, disappointment, or other things. We can skulk back to our beds of misery, anesthetize our pain with any of the addictions so prevalent today, and remain ignorant of our true selves; or we can choose not to waste the tailored, spiritual growth lab God has provided for us.

To be ignorant of our true selves means navigating our life's journey unconsciously without a spiritual compass and making decisions that lead us off our spiritual course into confusion and misdirection. In such a condition, our locus of control becomes external; we are subjugated to whatever or whoever exerts a pull on us. This is the *antithesis* of Wall-Seeking and Wall-Scaling.

An Ideal Spiritual Growth Medium

When our true self is spiritually attuned, however, our locus of control is internal. We decide what is important to us based on our recognition of the purposes of life and are open to guidance from our Maker. In this mode we strive to activate, develop, and express the divine qualities that lay latent within us.

The spiritual growth lab of life is providing us with the perfect environment, the ideal spiritual growth medium, to learn how to develop and manifest these latent virtues. The true self is *pre-wired* for this kind of existence; but each of us must exercise our free will, summon our energies, and make the choice to use the opportunities presented by the spiritual growth lab of life to achieve such an existence.

Chapter 6

The Spiritual Growth Lab of Life Is Calling Us to the Guided Condition

The third of the five truths that the Watchman Parable seems to teach us in order to better use our time on earth is that *the spiritual growth lab of life is calling us to the guided condition.*

The lover's awareness in the parable evolves from a sense of being lost and alone in a meaningless and impersonal world to a sense of being lovingly guided on a personal pathway by a loving Creator in a world infused with meaning. He also evolves from relying only on his own will to relying on the alignment of his own will with God's will for him. What is it that enables him to complete this evolution? We are told in the world's Holy Writings that God's mercy, grace, and guidance continually surround us, but that we have a part to play in accessing this bounty. The Hindu Writings emphasize that we must somehow take initiative.

> As men approach me, so I receive them. All paths, Arjuna, lead to me. [1]

The Muslim Writings emphasize our approach and obedience to God.

> O you who believe! Be mindful of your duty to God, and seek the way to approach unto Him, and strive in His way in order that you may succeed. [2]

The Writings of Judaism emphasize both trust in and acknowledgment of God.

> Trust in the Lord with all your heart, and do not rely
> on your own insight. In all your ways acknowledge
> Him and He will make straight your paths.[3]

The Christian Writings emphasize belief in and obedience to the divine Messenger.

> They said to him, "What must we do, to be doing
> the works of God?" Jesus answered them, "This is
> the work of God, that you believe in him whom he
> has sent."[4]

The Muslim Writings emphasize the condition of the heart and right action.

> Call on Him with fear and longing in your hearts:
> for the Mercy of God is near to those who do good.[5]

The Writings of the Bahá'í Faith emphasize preparation of the heart and the spirit.

> O Son of Being!
> Thy heart is My home; sanctify it for My descent.
> Thy spirit is My place of revelation; cleanse it
> for my manifestation.[6]

It is we who must strive to sanctify our hearts and cleanse our spirits in order to receive divine grace and guidance. Like a continuous radio wave, divine guidance and assistance are always there. But if the receiver is not clean, grounded, and unfettered, the guiding message can be missed or garbled by static.

The Sanctifying & Cleansing Process

Sanctifying and cleansing occurs when we work in a disciplined way to fulfill the three ultimate purposes of life; and it occurs when we adopt or intensify spiritual disciplines such as regular prayer, reading of scripture, meditation, serving others, fasting, and living according to divine teachings and commandments. Adopting such spiritual disciplines opens the channel of guidance in our hearts and spirits and attracts divine assistance. That each of us has the responsibility for proactively preparing ourselves to achieve and maintain such a guided condition is emphasized in the Holy Writings. The Judaic Writings suggest that developing faith is the key to guidance.

> Whoever has bread in his basket and says, "What am I going to eat tomorrow?" only belongs to those who are little in faith. [7]

The Christian Writings also emphasize faith, but add the specification of following divine teachings.

> Therefore do not be anxious, saying, "What shall we eat?" or "What shall we wear?" For the Gentiles seek all these things; and your heavenly Father knows that you need them all. But seek first his Kingdom and his righteousness, and all these things shall be yours as well. [8]

The Writings of Islam also stress faith and depict a proactive God.

> How many animals do not carry their own provision! God provides for them and for you. He is Alert, Aware. [9]

The Bahá'í Writings emphasize the personal responsibility each of us has in avoiding error and kindling faith in order to gain the guided condition.

> O My Friends:
>
> Quench ye the lamp of error, and kindle within your hearts the everlasting torch of divine guidance. [10]

The writings of Hinduism describe the process of purification we need to experience.

> Those who surrender to God all selfish attachments are like the leaf of a lotus floating clean and dry in water. Sin cannot touch them. Renouncing their selfish attachments, those who follow the path of service work with body, senses, and mind for the sake of self-purification.[11]

The Bahá'í Writings describe this purification process using a different metaphor.

> First in a human being's way of life must be purity, then freshness, cleanliness, and independence of spirit. First must the stream bed be cleansed, then may the sweet river waters be led into it. Chaste eyes enjoy the beatific vision of the Lord and know what this encounter meaneth; a pure sense inhaleth the fragrances that blow from the rose gardens of His grace; a burnished heart will mirror forth the comely face of truth.[12]

The tests and difficulties sent to us in life also provide opportunities to "burnish," cleanse, and sanctify our hearts so that we may adopt the guided condition. As painful as they can be and as hard as we may resist them, these tailored challenges come to us from God to stretch and guide us to more spiritual ways of thinking and behaving. Even though the lover in the parable initially resists any new learning, his tests and difficulties with the watchmen persist and gradually wear him down to the point that we find him "...forgetting his life..." and trusting in something beyond himself as he throws "...himself down to the garden." This is new behavior that leads to new insights. There on the other side of the wall, the lover's spiritual eyes open fully. He suddenly understands that to be in the guided condition he must trust God and align his will with God's will for him. To assist us and the lover in doing this, there are several additional principles the parable seems to teach us.

WALL-SEEKER PRINCIPLE:
There Is Guiding Intention in the Universe

At a very personal level, the Watchman Parable conveys that there is intention in the universe, and things are happening to you that are meant to guide you along a spiritual growth path. Although one could conclude from the basic story that the watchmen's influence is purely coincidental, the parable makes it plain that it is not coincidence but guidance. In response to the lover's affirmative exclamation, "For the watchman was Gabriel, guiding this poor one," the Narrator states, "Indeed his words were true, for he had found many a secret justice in this seeming tyranny of the watchman, and seen how many a mercy lay hid behind the veil." The message seems to be that there is purpose in the universe and in each individual life, and that these two purposes intertwine. Having this perspective is part of being in the guided condition.

WALL-SEEKER PRINCIPLE:
There Is Multiplicity of Guiding Intention in
the Universe

The Watchman Parable also conveys that there is *multiplicity* of guiding intention in the universe—things are happening to us and everyone around us that are meant to guide all of us along our individual spiritual growth paths. The climactic moment for the lover occurs after his decision to forget his life and throw himself over the wall into the garden below. The next paragraph begins, "And there he beheld his beloved with a lamp in her hand searching for a ring she had lost." Clearly, the beloved is also on a quest of her own, looking in the dust

"... searching for a ring she had lost." As a symbol, the ring suggests the completion, wholeness, or eternal meaning that the beloved is seeking in her own life. Like the lover, she has been on her own life path, with its attendant struggle, suffering, watchmen and choices, which have guided her to this very place in the garden. Seeing this multiplicity of intention is part of being in the guided condition.

WALL-SEEKER PRINCIPLE:
There Is Synchronicity Designed into Life

In addition, the Watchman Parable conveys that there is synchronicity designed into life. Synchronicity is the simultaneous and intersecting culmination of two or more apparently unrelated events to create a larger meaning. The parable seems to convey that things that happen to you to guide you along a spiritual growth path may be synchronized and intersect with things that are happening to someone else to guide them along a spiritual growth path. For example, maybe what we call chance or random meetings between people are no such thing, but represent unique opportunities for growth and development to both parties.

In the parable, such synchronicity is reflected in the simultaneous arrival of the lover and the beloved, each seeking fulfillment on their separate life paths, *at exactly the same spot, at exactly the same moment.* In a sense, one could say that at the moment when all seems lost, the hand of divine guidance makes its influence known, and both people's quests are unexpectedly and simultaneously fulfilled. Being mindful of and open to this kind of guided synchronicity is part of being in the guided condition.

WALL-SEEKER PRINCIPLE:
There Is Multiple Intentioned Synchronicity
Designed into Life

Since the characters in parables represent all of humankind, let us consider that what happened to the lover and the beloved is potentially happening to all of us, that synchronized spiritual growth path occurrences are happening to all people, and that our lives are intersecting in highly complex, multi-dimensional patterns. Within these patterns, we are the "lover" for some, the "beloved" for others, and "watchmen" for still others. In turn, others we encounter potentially play all these roles for us. So, while we go about our everyday lives running errands, doing our jobs, interacting with our children or significant other, or passing a stranger on the street, a larger drama may be at play.

In this wider context, those in watchmen roles are more than just supporting actors in the comprehensive drama. While a watchman bars the path to a lover, the watchman's actions are not only related to the lover's life path, but also to the watchman's own life path. On his own life path, the watchman is the central player and is recast as "the lover"; and the original lover is recast as "a watchman" that must be attended to. Their life paths are separate, but also intensely and mystically inter-connected.

When we take this larger view, the ramifications of all the guided individual dramas underway on the planet as they intersect with, and influence, each other create a vision too complex and awe-inspiring for human beings to fully comprehend. This vision reveals a God so powerful and loving that He simultaneously, and without omission, tends to the tailored spiritual growth needs of each of us and all of us. In the words of the Qur'án:

> No vision taketh in Him, but He taketh in all vision: and He is the Subtle, the All-informed. [13]

Being mindful of these larger spiritual growth patterns is part of being in the guided condition.

WALL-SEEKER PRINCIPLE:
Our Suffering Is Intended to Lead Us Away
from Self-Absorption & Limitation toward
Reliance on Divine Assistance & the Infinite

The Watchman Parable also suggests that the difficulties and suffering we experience in life are intended to lead us away from self-absorption and limitation and toward reliance on divine assistance and the infinite. When the lover is unwittingly "guided" by the watchmen to the wall, he has reached the dead-end of his reliance on self because, in that limited frame of reference, he is hemmed-in, cornered, and trapped. He has tried whatever he could think of on his own to relieve his suffering, but to no avail. Both figuratively and literally, the only directional movement available to him is to go *up* the wall.

By accepting the difficulties of climbing the wall, the lover moves into a new dimension away from the limited, self-contained perspective that has kept him locked in a pattern of flight from the watchmen. He moves toward new, more expansive terrain entailing an unknown future in which the possibilities are both boundless and hidden from him. By beginning to scale the wall, the lover has consciously or unconsciously stepped out of his familiar pattern toward something unfamiliar and less limited. And simply stepping into new, more limitless terrain seems to open the door to the guided condition and the lift of divine assistance that informs it. As evidence of this, the lover finds his strength augmented for the very difficult climb ahead of him.

Opening the door to the guided condition also seems to fuel his strength to do something entirely new when he reaches the top of the wall. After having been completely *attached* to the concept of self-preservation in response to the watchmen's challenges, the lover now uses his will power in a markedly *detached* way—"forgetting his life, he threw himself down to the garden." In this act he not only lets go of the life he has known, but spontaneously submits himself to something beyond himself—to divine assistance and the infinite. As a result, he discovers joy, release from his suffering, and faith in the reality of divine guidance and assistance.

Beyond the Watchman Parable, other Holy Writings also emphasize the importance of relying on divine assistance and the infinite as we encounter the vicissitudes of life. The Hindu Writings say:

> Abandon all supports and look to me for protection. I shall purify you from the sins of the past; do not grieve. [14]

The Jewish Writings say:

> He who submits himself to the yoke of the Torah liberates himself from the yoke of circumstance. He rises above the pressures of the state and above the fluctuations of worldly fortune. [15]

And:

> Make [God's] will as your will, So that He may make your will as His will. [16]

These sources, like the Watchman Parable, teach us that the sufferings inherent in spiritual growth are intended to release us from our limited, self-insistent ego and help us recognize that the key to this release is our own will. We simply need to *make the choice* to open the door to divine guidance and assistance. The lover in the parable is imprisoned in self-absorption when we first encounter him, but he evolves through his struggles and sufferings to the point where he learns to invite divine guidance and assistance into his life, and through them, find his beloved and access to the infinite.

In the Bahá'í Writings, 'Abdu'l-Bahá,[17] who spent over forty years in imprisonment and exile, says:

Unless one accepts dire vicissitudes, he will not attain. To me prison is freedom, troubles rest me, death is life, and to be despised is honor. Therefore, I was happy all that time in prison. When one is released from the prison of self, that is indeed release, for that is the greater prison. When this release takes place, then one cannot be outwardly imprisoned....The afflictions which come to humanity sometimes tend to center the consciousness upon the limitations, and this is a veritable prison. Release comes by making of the will a Door through which the confirmations of the Spirit come. [18]

The spiritual growth lab of life is trying to teach us to proactively *invite* the "confirmations of the Spirit" so that we can live in this guided condition to optimize our time on earth.

Chapter 7

The Spiritual Growth Lab of Life Is Calling Us Toward Spiritual Growth

The fourth of the five truths that the Watchman Parable seems to teach us, in order to better use our time on earth, is that *the spiritual growth lab of life is calling us toward spiritual growth.*

The end of the parable offers a perspective that can help us make the best use of life and maintain our equilibrium as we encounter difficulties.

> Now if the lover could have looked ahead, he would have blessed the watchman at the start, and prayed on his behalf, and he would have seen that tyranny as justice... those who journey in the garden-land of knowledge, because they see the end in the beginning, see peace in war and friendliness in anger.[1]

To "see the end in the beginning" may have many meanings, but one of them is to recognize that times of trouble are meant to take us to higher levels of awareness and understanding; and rather than despairing, it serves us to see that experiencing tests and difficulties, identifying walls, climbing over them with great difficulty, and discovering new awareness and understanding on the other side, is a pattern that is meant to be repeated in life for our own spiritual growth. This Wall-Seeking perspective acknowledges this repetitive pattern in the growth lab of life and welcomes it as a means to achieving continuous spiritual growth.

Let us look at some related wisdom in other Holy Writings that suggest we should welcome difficulties. In the Christian Writings, suffering is seen as something over which we should rejoice.

> **We rejoice in our sufferings, knowing that suffering produces endurance, and endurance produces character, and character produces hope, and hope does not disappoint us, because God's love has been poured into our hearts.** [2]

In the Buddhist Writings, troubles are seen as a "field of blessings."

> **Just as a great conflagration**
> **Can burn up all things,**
> **So does Buddha's field of blessings**
> **Burn up all fabrication.** [3]

In the Writings of Islam, trials are associated with the manifestation of gifts and attributes.

> **He has raised you in ranks, some above others, that He may try you in the gifts He has given you.** [4]

Elsewhere in the Bahá'í Writings, the value of proactively embracing the repetitive wall seeking and scaling pattern is confirmed.

> **The true lover yearneth for tribulation even as doth the rebel for forgiveness and the sinful for mercy.** [5]

WALL-SEEKER PRINCIPLE:
We Should Welcome the Watchmen in Our
Lives

If we are going to make tribulation our friend, we must begin by welcoming the watchmen in our lives. Watchmen tend to block or disrupt us in some way and may take the shape of a family member, a loved one, a co-worker, a customer, a stranger, a vendor, a teacher, a student, a law officer, a friend, an enemy, someone in the helping professions, a government worker, a pet, or even a repetitive thought within the mind. Watchmen are not always animate; they can also be circumstances such as a promotion, a firing, being passed over for a promotion, an accident, an illness, a disrupting schedule change, or a frustrating pattern we experience in our lives. Sometimes watchmen show up in pairs or groups; for example, one could be simultaneously disrupted by a critical statement from a loved one, being passed over for a promotion, and a repetitive thought within one's mind—all of which point to some area of one's life where change and growth are needed. Welcoming such watchmen into our lives and awareness is usually not easy.

The lover in the Watchman Parable demonstrates the change we must make when he evolves in his attitude toward the watchmen from seeing them initially as enemies to finally blessing them as guides. The parable also suggests that it is a waste of time and energy to try to determine if the watchmen we encounter are motivated by love or wrath. The parable clarifies this when it says:

> **Indeed his words were true, for he had found many a secret justice in this seeming tyranny of the watchman, and seen how many a mercy lay hid behind the veil. Out of wrath, the guard had led him who was athirst in love's desert to the sea of his loved one, and lit up the dark night of absence with the light of reunion. He had driven one who was afar, into the garden of nearness, had guided an ailing soul to the heart's physician.** [6]

Whether the watchmen in our lives are motivated by wrath or love is irrelevant—they are still meant to guide us. What may appear as "tyranny" is actually "a secret justice." The appearance of a watchman means that the spiritual growth lab of life is trying to get our attention. If we want to be wise wayfarers on the path of change and spiritual growth, we need to see the watchmen as guides from the beginning; and we need to reflect on their significance to our lives regardless of how they present themselves—whether they convey love, anger, curiosity, sarcasm, animosity, humor, indifference, condescension, compassion, or some other emotion.

WALL-SEEKER PRINCIPLE:
The Goal Is to Quickly Identify & Scale the Walls in Our Lives

---

To be enlightened then, we must proactively look for the watchmen in our lives, identify the walls in our lives the watchmen are guiding us to, and willingly approach and scale those walls in order to expedite increased understanding and spiritual growth. The final paragraph of the Watchman Parable contrasts the enlightened one who *seeks* watchmen and walls and the unenlightened one who *avoids* them.

> Now if the lover could have looked ahead, he would have blessed the watchman at the start, and prayed on his behalf, and he would have seen that tyranny as justice; but since the end was veiled to him, he moaned and made his plaint in the beginning.[7]

By welcoming watchmen as guides, we can more quickly use them to identify the next walls we need to scale and shorten the cycle time to get over each wall. Our true selves are motivated to accelerate this process because they are attracted to spiritual growth and ever-increasing nearness to the ultimate Beloved, the Creator. The Holy Writings encourage such speed. The Buddhist writings say:

> Make haste in doing good; check your mind from
> evil; for the mind of him who is slow in doing mer-
> itorious actions delights in evil....Should a person
> perform meritorious action, he should do it again
> and again; he should find pleasure therein: blissful
> is the accumulation of merit. [8]

And the Bahá'í Writings say:

> Be swift in the path of holiness, and enter the heav-
> en of communion with Me. Cleanse thy heart with
> the burnish of the spirit, and hasten to the court of
> the Most High. [9]

Watchmen, or difficulties and tests that present opportunities for growth, are not always easily recognized; and the walls they are trying to guide us to scale are sometimes even more difficult to recognize. To identify watchmen in our individual lives, for example, we may need to become aware of fear, anger, anxiety, or resentment we are harboring, and this will require us to take an honest inventory of what we are struggling with. Walls we need to scale could be things such as: learning to acknowledge our intelligence; learning to acknowledge other people's intelligence; accepting our right to exist or achieve success; believing in our capacity to love or be loved; committing to advancing our education; getting a different job, or starting a business; claiming our health and well-being; stepping away from self-centeredness and beginning to be of service to others; developing our capacity for faith; or innumerable other things. Often the wall we need to scale is the most difficult thing we can think of that would significantly foster our growth.

When we consider that the dynamics described in the Watchman Parable are not only relevant to individual spiritual growth, but to the spiritual growth of couples, families, organizations, communities, states, nations, and humankind as a whole, we realize that building skills in watchmen and wall recognition is essential. Individually and collectively, if we bring Wall-Seeking qualities to the issues and problems we encounter, the achievement of spiritual growth and higher understanding will be accelerated. So, for example, instead of choosing blame and contention (within oneself or interpersonally), the Wall-Seeker mind-set asks questions such as: *What are the watchmen forces that seem to be working on me/us? What wall do I/we sense I am/we are supposed to scale? What is the beloved that I/we seek? What am I/are we to learn from this? What are life's events trying to teach me/us? What is trying to happen here?* Conflict and contention are thereby transformed into a collaborative process in which each perspective honors and contributes to the change and spiritual growth patterns of all.

WALL-SEEKER PRINCIPLE:
*The Key to Aligning Doing & Being in Our
Lives Is Seeing the End in the Beginning*

Knowing ourselves involves being able to separate in our minds our "doing" and our "being." *Doing* has to do with the actions we take in our lives while *being* has to do with the qualities and attributes we bring to our actions. For example, if someone asked, "What are you *doing* in your life?" you might say, "I am a manager at XYZ Co., I am a stay-at-home mom/dad, I am a student, or I am a botanist," etc. But answering the question "Who are you *being* in your life?" involves thinking about the attributes that characterize your *being* while you have been *doing*.

The nature of our *doing* and *being* are two primary life choices we make. One way of thinking about spiritual growth is to see it as increasing the alignment—that is, decreasing the hypocrisy or misalignment—between our doing and being. For example, if I am a manager who expects my employees to *be* honest, hard-working, and fair, I must strive to manifest these qualities *in action* myself. If, as a parent, I tell my children to be kind and accepting of others, I must work to be kind and accepting of my children and others as well. When I achieve this increased alignment between my being and doing, I have grown spiritually and become a more authentic human being.

The spiritual growth lab of life gives us repeated opportunities to do the hard work required to increase the alignment between our doing and being. The motivation to do this difficult work springs from recognition of the three ultimate purposes of life—to know and love God, to develop spiritual attributes, and to carry forward an ever-advancing civilization. If we see these three purposes as the "end" or desired outcomes in terms of our *being*, then we know better how to go about our *doing* in life. As it is said in the Watchman Parable, we "see the end in the beginning" and this changes our approach to life.

In the beginning of the parable, the central character is a limited lover and seeker; his loving and seeking are directed only toward the beloved. Toward the watchmen and his Creator, he shows neither the *being* attribute of love nor the investigatory *doing* qualities of a seeker. The limitation of, and misalignment between, the lover's doing and being complicates his life and lengthens his search. However, in the climactic scene of the parable when the lover goes over the wall and beholds his beloved, his spiritual eye fully opens, and he sees "the end in the beginning." He sees the spiritual *purposes* behind the tests, difficulties, struggles, and choices that his life journey has presented to him. And in that moment, rather than being exclusively occupied with the limited *doing* of loving and celebrating his beloved, the lover finds his *doing* to be widened to include the loving and celebrating of the watchmen and, in particular, his Creator. He has grown in his ability to know and love God. In addition, he finds his *doing* qualities to be aligned with the *being* attributes of compassion, awe, reverence, prayerfulness, gratitude, humility, generosity of spirit, and justice. The lover has developed spiritual attributes that were previously only latent within him. And in his recognition and valuing of all the collaborating role-players—of Creator, watchmen, beloved, and lover—in the spiritually-centered growth drama, the lover has become a contributor to the advancement of civilization. His being and doing are now aligned with the three ultimate purposes of life, enabling him to "see the end in the beginning," and this changes the lover's perspective on, and approach to, life. He recognizes the desired outcomes for his life in this material realm, and that he must be alert to, and seek to further leverage, the kind of human interaction and spiritual growth patterns he has just experienced.

The Search for the Beloved

The dynamics of change and spiritual growth described in the Watchman Parable are constantly at play in each person's lifetime. The "beloved" that is sought can refer to whatever brings fulfillment, meaning, peace, and contentment. At its most sacred level, the search for the beloved represents each person's search for God. This is confirmed in the Holy Writings. As referenced earlier, in the Judaic Writings, God says:

> Then shall ye call upon me, and ye shall go and pray unto me, and I will hearken unto you. And ye shall seek me, and find me, when ye shall search for me with all your heart.[10]

Also as previously referenced, in the Christian Writings, Jesus Christ says:

> Ask, and it shall be given you; seek, and ye shall find; knock, and it shall be opened unto you: For every one that asketh receiveth; and he that seeketh findeth; and to him that knocketh it shall be opened.[11]

And in the Bahá'í Writings, Bahá'u'lláh says:

> Blessed is the wayfarer who hath recognized the Desired One, and the seeker who hath heeded the Call of Him Who is the intended Aim of all mankind, and the learned one who hath believed in God, the Help in Peril, the Self-Subsisting.[12]

Other searches for the beloved in our lives are implicit in questions such as: Who do I want to become? What will I value and honor? What qualities in a significant other will help me to develop in meaningful ways? How can I earn a living while honoring my God-given talents? How will I serve? How will I parent? And how will I keep growing during my time on earth? Our answers to such questions in pursuit of our beloveds are critically important because they will either better align us or further misalign us with the three purposes of life.

The nature of the beloved itself may also evolve in terms of these three purposes. For example, early in our careers we may see the beloved as "finding a job." A few years later, the beloved may be "finding a job that pays better." Several years after that, the beloved may be "finding a job that I enjoy." And ultimately, the beloved in terms of career may be "finding or creating the job that best helps me fulfill the three purposes of life." Clearly, if our beloveds are evolving over time, the ideal is to have them moving from the more superficial to the more profound, rather than the other way around.

Individual & Group Change & Spiritual Growth

Because spiritual growth requires change and change requires effort, understanding the change process can help mitigate frustration and impatience. Change that leads to spiritual growth involves a process of replacing one learned response to a situation with a different and better response to the same situation. A better response would be one that more fully honors the three purposes of life—knowing and loving God, developing spiritual attributes, and carrying forward an ever-advancing civilization. The change could be aimed at the *doing* level, the *being* level, or both. It could also be at the *individual* level, the *group* level, or both.

An Individual Example of Change & Spiritual Growth

Let's look at an *individual* change example. Mary has learned how to drive to her job each day (at the *doing* level) and experiences considerable frustration (at the *being* level) with the traffic during the commute. One morning she starts off to work and discovers that a long-term detour has been put in place. Over the next several days she learns how to make different decisions in response to the challenge of how to get to work (an advance at the *doing* level), but experiences even more intense frustration, anger, and impatience with the commute (a regression at the *being* level). In this scenario, while Mary has mastered some change and has grown at the *doing* level, it would be difficult to argue that she has experienced spiritual growth.

An alternative scenario would have her learning the new route (an advance at the *doing* level) and, through an act of will, deciding to manifest greater patience and tranquility during the commute (an advance at the *being* level). To accomplish this change in *being*, Mary might need to practice deep breathing or muscle relaxation behind the wheel. When the traffic is very slow, she could use some of her energy to pray for patience and tranquility and to meditate on these attributes. Mary could also cultivate resignation and submission to a situation over which she has no control; and she would benefit from learning to replace her anger with compassion for the other drivers who are experiencing the same powerlessness that she is. In making all of these changes, Mary would be more fully honoring the three purposes of life; and in all likelihood, the changes would positively impact other segments of her life as well.

Advances at the being or doing levels that more fully honor the three purposes of life represent spiritual growth. In the latter scenario, Mary has used the detour problem in the material realm as a vehicle for growth in the spiritual realm. This is similar to what the lover learns to do in the Watchman Parable. In the words of the parable, Mary is: looking ahead and accepting, if not blessing, the watchmen (the detour, the traffic, and other individual drivers) at the start for providing an opportunity to develop greater patience, tranquility, submission, resignation, and compassion; seeing the end (or purposes of life) in the beginning; and seeing peace in war and friendliness in anger. Indeed, these kinds of everyday situations offer opportunities for spiritual growth when the Wall-Seeking perspective is present.

A Group Example of Change & Spiritual Growth

Group settings offer opportunities for change as well. Let's look at a *group* change example. A group encounters a problem and convenes a meeting to address it. During the meeting, the group arrives at a solution (an advance at the *doing* level), but in the process of both reaching the decision and implementing it in the organization, relationships become strained, and disrespect, distrust, and disunity are increased (a regression at the collective *being* level). It would be difficult to argue that the group has grown spiritually at this point.

An alternative scenario would have the group convening, solving the problem together (an advance at the *doing* level), and in the process of both reaching the decision and implementing it in the organization, harmonizing relationships and increasing respect, justice, trust, knowledge, compassion, service, and unity (an advance at the collective *being* level). In this scenario, the group has strengthened spiritual attributes within the organization; and it has enhanced organizational unity, which represents an advance in a component of civilization. Once again, a*dvances in being or doing at the group level that more fully honor the three purposes of life represent spiritual growth.*

The interpersonal dynamics within groups make it possible for spiritual growth to occur at the group level *and* the individual level simultaneously. In the latter scenario, the group and the individuals in it have successfully used a problem in the material realm as a vehicle for growth in the spiritual realm. This, too, is similar to what the lover learns to do in the Watchman Parable. In the words of the parable, the group and its members are looking ahead. They are: accepting, if not blessing, the watchmen (the problem facing the group) at the start for providing an opportunity to create not just a solution strategy, but one that aligns with spiritual values; seeing the end (or purposes of life) in the beginning; and seeing peace in war and friendliness in anger. Indeed, these kinds of everyday group situations offer opportunities for spiritual growth when the Wall-Seeking perspective is present.

A Model of Change & Spiritual Growth

In the two scenarios above, where an individual and a group decide to choose spiritual growth, we see the *process* and *outcomes* of their growth choices, not the *internal mechanics* required to make the choices. The following **Basic Model of Change and Spiritual Growth** emphasizes the conscious effort required to successfully change and grow. [13]

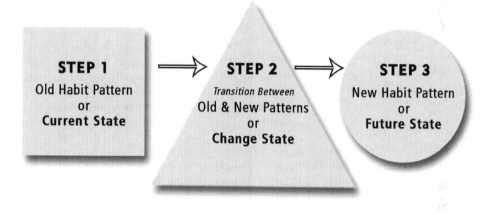

In **Step 1** of this diagram, which represents the **Current State**, we are responding to a given stimulus with **an old habit pattern** that is no longer serving us. Nevertheless, the current state is characterized by stable conditions (our habit pattern produces stable and consistent responses), predictability (we know what to expect), and certainty (we exercise our habitual response with no deliberate thought and can rely on the usual results). Minimal learning, change, and growth are taking place.

In **Step 2**, the **Change State**, we begin reacting to the same stimulus with a **new response**. The change state is characterized by unstable conditions (our new response produces unstable and inconsistent reactions), unpredictability and variability (we don't know what to expect), and uncertainty (we exercise our new response using very deliberate thought and get uncertain results). Extensive learning, change, and growth are taking place.

In **Step 3**, the **Future State**, we are responding to the given stimulus with **the new habit pattern** that is serving us more effectively. The future state is characterized by stable conditions (our new habit pattern produces stable and consistent reactions), predictability (we know what to expect), and certainty (we exercise our new habit with no deliberate thought and can rely on improved results). Once again, little learning, change, and growth are taking place. **However, the Future State becomes the Current State for the next round of change and spiritual growth.**

The Swamp of Change & Spiritual Growth

The foregoing description of the three steps may make the change process sound simple and inevitable. The fact is that *huge amounts of effort* must be expended to navigate through Step 2; and change efforts are usually accompanied by a great deal of struggle, stretching, regression, recommitment, failure, and ultimately success. Step 2 (the change state), the transition between the old and new habit pattern, is the place where our dissatisfaction and frustration with the old habit pattern (the current state) has led us to struggle to make a change and grow beyond it. During Step 2, the new habit pattern (the future state) is not yet in place. Like the lover during most of the Watchman Parable, we are struggling between two worlds, the "what was" and the "what will be."

Years ago one of our professional colleagues, Alan Scheffer, [14] likened this in-between state to crossing a swamp. Indeed, we often refer to Step 2 as the *Swamp of Change and Spiritual Growth,* because completing Step 2 is very much like crossing a swamp. Without question, you will get wet and muddy. You will slip, stumble, and fall. Despite your efforts to be graceful, you will be awkward and clumsy. Your feet will feel heavy and, to get across the swamp to Step 3 (the new habit pattern or future state), you will have to continue despite fatigue, frustration, and sometimes despair.

The Swamp of Change—A Universal Dynamic

It is important to keep in mind that the "swamp of change" dynamics apply to individual, group, organizational, community, and global change. If a family resolves to start having sit-down dinners together each evening *without* the television on, the transition struggle to disengage from the old habit and establish the new habit will be similar. Likewise, if the sales manager in an organization resolves to begin meeting with his sales team each Friday morning to deepen knowledge and skills and report on progress and opportunities in the field, the transition struggle from the condition of "not meeting" to the condition of "consistently meeting" will be similarly challenging for the manager and the salespeople. Similarly, if two warring factions, regions, or nations determine to establish peace and collaborative relationships, the transition struggle from seeing each other as adversaries to accepting each other as partners will be swamp-like in all respects.

Learning to Embrace the Swamp & the Walls

We have been culturally conditioned to dislike and avoid the stress and untidiness of the swamp of change and growth. Not only does our culture train us to seek quick and easy solutions that cause us as little discomfort as possible, but it encourages us to present ourselves as graceful, clean, and in control rather than as awkward, muddy, humbled, and disoriented. Accordingly, like ducks that appear to glide smoothly and effortlessly across the water while their legs and feet beat furiously against the currents, we try to hide and minimize whatever struggles we are having. Furthermore, contemporary communication media tend to overload our senses, preoccupy us with trivial, purposeless distractions, and induce in us passivity, lethargy, and the desire to be entertained rather than the energy and discipline necessary to grapple with personal and collective change and spiritual growth.

However, if we want to use our brief time on earth to grow in the ways we are supposed to grow, *we need to embrace the walls and the swamp.* It is our challenge, once we have experienced and acknowledged the swamp, to become familiar with it, welcome it, and even find beauty in it. Like the Seminole Tribe of Native Americans who were harassed and chased many years ago into the forbidding swamps of the Florida Everglades, we can learn not only to survive in the swamp, but to thrive and flourish there. When we welcome the swamp and the walls in our lives, we do so because we know that is where the learning and growth are, and we yearn to reach the more advanced levels of doing and being on the other side.

The Basic Change & Spiritual Growth Model as a Pattern for Scaling Walls

The Basic Change & Spiritual Growth Model identifies a spiritual growth pattern for Wall-Seekers. Scaling walls—that is, surmounting tests and difficulties—in our lives involves the movement from the Current State through the Change State to the Future State. The Watchman Parable begins with the lover suffering in the Current State. When he leaves his house for the marketplace, he embarks on a journey through the Change State. And after scaling the wall and landing in the garden, he finds himself in the Future State. For the lover and ourselves, if we navigate through these three states in alignment with the three purposes of life, we are not only going over walls but achieving spiritual growth.

WALL-SEEKER PRINCIPLE:
To Change & Grow Spiritually, It Helps to
Follow A Sequence of:

1. Taking action to engage with others or
our self on the issue;

2. Becoming humble & submissive in
response to God's guidance;

3. Making ourselves vulnerable, detaching from life as we know it, and climbing with difficulty toward a higher spiritual dimension;

4. Being willing to sacrifice, making a signal act of faith, and trusting in divine guidance.

The Watchman Parable provides clues about actions and attributes that expedite the change and spiritual growth process.

Taking Action to Engage with Others or Our Self on the Issue

The first of these clues is taking action to engage with others or our self on the issue we are facing. Nothing changes for the lover until he arises from his bed of misery and moves with his issue toward the marketplace where he encounters the watchmen. The marketplace can be seen as a central venue of the spiritual growth lab of life because it provides an intersection for the exchange of thoughts, goods, services, feelings, and ideas; and engaging with these things—whether interpersonally (in terms of interactions with others) or intra-personally (in terms of interactions within our self)—tends to trigger insights into the watchmen dynamics in our lives and consequent change.

Becoming Humble & Submissive in Response to God's Guidance

The parable suggests that two attributes that expedite the change and spiritual growth process are humility and submission in response to God's guidance. Through most of the parable, the lover is anything but humble and submissive. He asserts his own will, is not mindful of divine guidance, assumes he knows better than the watchmen what is best for him, and refuses to submit to their forces. Nevertheless, his struggles gradually wear him down and ripen him for the change and spiritual growth ahead. He does not fully manifest humility and submission until he is on the other side of the wall and is able to "see the end in the beginning." Suddenly, the lover is humbled by the recognition that a loving God has been influencing the watchmen forces to facilitate his growth and discovery of the beloved; and he realizes that in the future, he must humbly "look ahead" and submit himself willingly to the watchmen forces in order to more rapidly discover the walls they reveal.

Other Holy Writings also confirm the importance of humility and submission in response to divine guidance. The Christian Writings say:

> Whoever exalts himself will be humbled, and whoever humbles himself will be exalted. [15]

In the Bahá'í Writings, God says:

> Humble thyself before Me, that I may graciously visit thee. [16]

Making Ourselves Vulnerable

When we make any move toward significant change in life, we experience vulnerability. Moving into new terrain brings fears that we could lose control, look silly, appear incompetent, or fail miserably. Skillfully navigating change requires that we quiet our insistent egos (which favor safety and the status quo), engage our true selves (which hunger for spiritual growth), and accept the risks of moving into unknown territory.

In the process of going to the marketplace, the lover in the Watchman Parable initially resists making himself vulnerable and defensively wrestles with what he perceives to be the antagonism of the watchmen. Only when he starts scaling the wall with great difficulty does he willingly begin accepting the vulnerability associated with moving into new terrain. When he reaches the top of the wall and then throws himself into the darkness of the garden below, he fully embraces his vulnerability. As a result, he discovers his beloved, recognizes the compassionate purpose of his Creator, and realizes that in the future he must *intentionally* open himself and make himself vulnerable to the influence of new forces as a pre-requisite for accelerating spiritual growth.

Detaching from Life as We Know It

Spiritual growth requires an increase in spiritual awareness, which usually entails seeing more dimensions, nuance, subtlety, and meaning in existence. Such growth often requires letting go of a narrow perspective in order to gain a wider, more meaningful perspective. The Watchman Parable suggests that we must detach from life as we know it in order to step into a higher spiritual dimension.

Through most of the parable, the lover is holding tightly to his habitual frame of reference. He is defensively acting and reacting without deliberation or expansion of his awareness. He is trying path after path to achieve his desire, but there is no increase in his *being* attributes to inform his *doing*. He is focused on *worldly*, not *spiritual*, reality. The lover could stay indefinitely in this defensive posture. A defensive posture favors the status quo; it is a form of attachment to the current state that blocks progression through the change state to the future state. A defensive posture also prevents the emergence of higher awareness. Every passageway the lover encounters is seen by him solely as an avenue for avoidance of the watchmen and continued attachment to self-preservation. He is still firmly attached to his life as he knows it.

However, the dynamics of change and spiritual growth inherent in the growth lab of life progressively discourage the lover from clinging to the status quo and his habitual frame of reference. Watchmen continue to emerge at every turn so that change avoidance and attachment to his life as he knows it become increasingly difficult to maintain. He is left with no means of escape within his current frame of reference. The change and growth dynamics *pry the lover's grip loose* from his life until, at the top of the wall, he finds himself "forgetting his life." Only then is he ready to throw himself into the garden of new awareness.

Climbing with Difficulty toward a Higher Spiritual Dimension

The Watchman Parable also suggests that, in order to change and grow, we must move, step, or climb with difficulty toward a higher spiritual dimension that we may not be able to define until we have arrived there. The garden wall in the parable can be seen as the transition point between the lover's current level of development and a higher spiritual dimension to which he is being called. Walls, or obstacles, by their nature, require that we either content ourselves with the boundaries they establish or *raise ourselves higher* to climb over them and discover what is on the other side. The parable tells us that such walls are meant to be scaled, but that scaling them can entail "untold pain." When the lover in the parable starts *raising himself higher* by climbing the wall that separates him from a higher spiritual dimension, the pain and the effort required of him intensify. And, it is not until the lover lands on the other side of the wall and beholds his beloved that he has clarity about the nature of the new spiritual dimension he has reached.

Being Willing to Sacrifice, Making a Signal Act of Faith, & Trusting In Guidance

Sacrifice can be thought of as the willingness to give up the important for the more important; and sacrifice informs spiritual growth. The lover's willingness to sacrifice in the Watchman Parable begins haltingly with his letting go of the two-dimensional attempt to escape laterally from the watchmen (he has been running only east and west or north and south). This sacrifice is necessary in order for him to see the garden wall as a viable escape route in a new, third dimension—upward. His willingness to sacrifice expands a little more with his commitment to actually scale the entire wall regardless of how high and difficult it proves to be. He is giving up the challenging "known" for the even more challenging "unknown."

Having arrived at the top of the garden wall, the lover has progressed to a state where he is willing to sacrifice any notion of safety and self-preservation in order to try to change his condition. He is now willing to give up everything in the path of his escape from the watchmen and his quest for the beloved; and he makes a preliminary, but signal, act of faith ("and forgetting his life, he threw himself down to the garden"). A "signal" act of faith is something striking and distinct from a person's usual behavior.

At this stage of the lover's development, the signal act of faith is throwing himself into the hands of something outside himself. He throws himself into the darkness of the unknown and gives up control. He is not so much trusting in divine guidance at this point as demonstrating freedom from whatever he has trusted before; and this is the first step toward trusting in divine guidance.

Moments later, however, after discovering his beloved, becoming "the heart-surrendered lover," and recognizing God's hand in all that has transpired, the lover understands more fully the dynamics of change and spiritual growth. He realizes: the importance of scaling walls with great difficulty, of *proactively* sacrificing one's self in the path of a great quest, goal, or longing; of making a signal act of faith by stepping forward in the night when one cannot see a pathway; and of trusting that there is a compassionate purpose animating the universe that will guide and break one's fall into the dark unknown.

Climbing Over Walls & Spiritual Attainment

The dynamics of the spiritual growth lab of life and related clues from the Watchman Parable speak to all of our personal lives. When watchmen forces tell us that we are not growing, that what we have been doing is not helping us to be the person God wants us to be, we have come to a wall. On the other side of this wall is a beloved of some kind, the attainment of which will fill us with joy. We can decide to remain stuck and stay with the familiar rut we are in; or we can decide to change. This is where growth can occur if we open ourselves to transformation. This is where the lover in the parable, after much suffering, gives up control and lets go of the familiar. He gives up the challenging known for the even more challenging unknown. He wades into the swamp of change.

Beyond the specific beloveds we may seek, the watchmen and wall forces are often challenging us to more effectively fulfill the three purposes of life. For example, the wall we must scale may require us to reach inside ourselves to find a latent quality, capacity, or spiritual attribute that we have not used, but which we need to manifest in order to grow. The reader will recall that Chapter 1 cited examples from the Holy Writings that challenge us to develop divine attributes: that we "must be perfect as your Heavenly Father is perfect"; [17] that we are "God's Temple"; [18] that we have "gems" hidden within us that we need to "lay bare." [19] The wall-scaling work before us, then, may be to bring forth the God-given attributes that lie latent within us— such as patience, forgiveness, or humility—so that they become part of our character.

Or the watchmen and wall forces may be challenging us to reach inside ourselves in order to better carry forward an ever-advancing civilization. For example, we know God wants us to love others, so perhaps we need to reach out in friendship to people of a different religion, race, or culture, to ask God to help us get beyond any narrowness, conventionality, or prejudice so that we can habitually express the acceptance, appreciation, love, and compassion that will help unify society.

Other examples of advancing civilization by going over walls might include deciding to patch up a relationship with a family member or friend, volunteering to do something to serve others, giving up hypocrisy—saying one thing and doing another, renouncing criticism and blame and instead cultivating acceptance and compassion for others and yourself. As we strive to do such things, we learn to trust that God will guide us and help us activate the latent virtues we need to navigate this new territory. We also learn to accept our vulnerability, anticipate hardship, detach from our lives as we have known them, sacrifice safety, and advance toward known and unknown beloveds that will bring us great joy.

When we have the faith and courage to proactively scale our walls and throw ourselves down into the darkness on the other side, we not only use the spiritual growth lab of life effectively, we experience new understanding. We find ourselves in a land of higher awareness. Like Dorothy opening the door of her house after landing in Oz, we see a new reality with new eyes and realize we are no longer in Kansas. Because walls relate to spiritual awareness, going over them typically represents an advance in the realm of spiritual understanding that can immediately inform our *being* and *doing* in the next stages of our spiritual growth.

Chapter 8

The Spiritual Growth Lab of Life Is Calling Us Toward Collaborative Rather Than Adversarial Human Interactions

So far, we have said that the spiritual growth lab of life is calling us toward spiritual reality, calling forth our true self, calling us to the guided condition, and calling us toward spiritual growth. The fifth of the five truths that the Watchman Parable seems to teach us in order to better use our time on earth is that *the spiritual growth lab of life is calling us toward accessing divine assistance followed by collaborative rather than adversarial human interactions to resolve life issues.*

The final paragraph of the parable gives us a vision of the lover's evolution in understanding as he progresses through the Valley of Knowledge.

> Now if the lover could have looked ahead, he would have blessed the watchman at the start, and prayed on his behalf, and he would have seen that tyranny as justice; but since the end was veiled to him, he moaned and made his plaint in the beginning. Yet those who journey in the garden-land of Knowledge, because they see the end in the beginning, see peace in war and friendliness in anger. [1]

This vision has many dimensions. Significant among them is that the lover seems to have reached a higher level of understanding regarding how to approach personal and inter-personal issues and challenges in life.

When the parable begins, the lover has a serious issue—he is wasting "in the fire of remoteness." In an effort to address his issue, he finds himself coming into reluctant engagement with others (the watchmen) and contends with them in an adversarial fashion, seeing them as obstacles, enemies, and antagonists. He generates and expends great amounts of negative energy—moaning, blaming, and complaining—while contending with the watchmen and attempting to control circumstances. Contention of this type is a primitive form of interaction, less primitive than war, but not very different from partisan politics or adversarial debate in which the other party is vilified and portrayed as a misguided barrier to progress.

Only after going over the wall does the lover realize that "the end was veiled to him," that he has completely misread the situation, that the watchmen—regardless of their demeanor—have advanced rather than retarded his progress, and that the *interpenetration* of their influence, his influence, and God's hand have guided the lover to the resolution of his issue. Now, standing with his beloved on the far side of the wall, seeing the watchmen as angels rather than tyrants, filled with compassion, and inclined to bless "the watchman at the start" and pray "on his behalf," the lover recognizes that he must "see the end in the beginning" and address issues differently in the future. In order to most effectively resolve issues, deepen understanding and generate spiritual growth, he must simultaneously *call on God's guidance* and *collaborate with the watchmen* so that *the influence of all three—God, watchmen, and lover—can interpenetrate* to optimize his decision-making and accelerate his path to his beloved. In dealing with the watchmen in particular, he must cling persistently to "peace," "friendliness," and "justice" in exchanges that would earlier have triggered "anger" and thoughts of "war" or "tyranny" in him. This is because any watchman's demeanor may appear to contradict the role he is actually playing to guide the lover to the beloved.

The subject of how to most effectively interact, deliberate, and decide is touched upon in other Holy Writings. In the Judaic Writings, God seems to pose a path of interaction, reasoning, and decision-making that is a more mature alternative to various destructive forms of adversarial warring and conflict.

> **Come now, and let us reason together, saith the Lord: though your sins be as scarlet, they shall be as white as snow; though they be red like crimson, they shall be as wool.**
>
> **If ye be willing and obedient, ye shall eat the good of the land.**
>
> **But if you refuse and rebel, ye shall be devoured with the sword; for the mouth of the Lord hath spoken it. [2]**

In addition to suggesting that if we reason together collaboratively, we can turn guilt and resentment into forgiveness and a new beginning ("…though your sins be as scarlet, they shall be as white as snow."), this passage also seems to convey that God wants to be a participant in our "reasoning together." The passage is an ancient one which demonstrates that human beings have been grappling for a long time with the alternatives of "reasoning together" with the involvement of God through prayer, or being "devoured with the sword" in destructive contention, conflict, and battle. More recently in human history, the Islamic Writings raise the same issue and then praise those "…whose affairs are guided by mutual counsel." [3]

In the modern era, the Bahá'í Writings introduce an optimal human interaction process called "consultation" to be used for deepening understanding, solving problems, and making decisions. Consultation involves first praying for divine assistance and then deliberating collaboratively and compassionately—with members of a group or with aspects of one's inner being—to reach wise and unifying decisions on the most important and difficult issues of life.

The Bahá'í Writings say:

> Take ye counsel together in all matters, inasmuch as consultation is the lamp of guidance which leadeth the way, and is the bestower of understanding.[4]

And:

> The heaven of divine wisdom is illumined with the two luminaries of consultation and compassion.[5]

And:

> Therefore, true consultation is spiritual conference in the attitude and atmosphere of love. Members [of the group] must love each other in the spirit of fellowship in order that good results may be forthcoming. Love and fellowship are the foundation.[6]

And:

> No welfare and no well-being can be attained except through consultation.[7]

Taken together, these weighty scriptural statements from the ancient to the recent past make it clear that *improving the way we interact and decide* is part of the divine curriculum in the spiritual growth lab of life. And the advance of humankind through the successive levels and grades in this curriculum has now given us access to "consultation," an advanced human interaction process that we can now learn to apply. This forms the basis of another Wall-Seeker principle.

WALL-SEEKER PRINCIPLE:
In Resolving Issues, Collaborative Consultation Informed by Divine Assistance Results in Greater Understanding & Spiritual Growth Than Does Adversarial Contention

---

The consultation process is ideal for Wall-Seekers because it expedites achieving spiritual growth and the three purposes of life while grappling with the resolution of typical worldly issues and problems. Because a full treatment of the consultation process is beyond the scope of this book, it will be only briefly introduced in this and the last chapter; however, it is the entire focus of our next book.

For our purposes in this chapter, we simply suggest that an effective way of using consultation as a Wall-Seeker entails praying for divine assistance before all significant decisions and then posing and answering the following set of questions in a compassionate and collaborative atmosphere.

Wall-Seeking Questions to Stimulate Consultation Decision-Making

1. How do my/our present circumstances relate to my/our ultimate life purposes?

2. What and/or who are the Watchmen in my/our life/lives and where are their forces leading me/us?

3. What is the Wall that I/we need to scale and go over?

4. What spiritual principles need to influence my/our search for the beloved?

5. What is the beloved for which I/we am/are longing?

6. What are the steps to the beloved that align with the spiritual principles?

While our next book will attempt to thoroughly explore the features, processes, and approaches to consultation, as an assistance to readers of the present book we include the following passage from the Bahá'í Writings, describing the atmosphere and process that need to inform the interpenetration of ideas during consultation.

> They [the group] must, when coming together, turn their faces to the Kingdom on high and ask aid from the Realm of Glory. They must then proceed with the utmost devotion, courtesy, dignity, care and moderation to express their views. They must in every matter search out the truth and not insist upon their own opinion, for stubbornness and persistence in one's views will lead ultimately to discord and wrangling and the truth will remain hidden. [8]

This quotation has obvious implications for group settings, but it and the Watchman Parable can also be seen to have implications for using consultation within the individual.

The Watchman Parable & Consulting Within the Self

The lover in the parable not only wrestles with the watchmen, but with the different voices inside his own head. One voice would have him remain isolated and safe, another would have him move toward the marketplace, another still would have him contend with the watchmen, and still another would have his heart lament and reframe his experiences. Even the watchmen themselves may be seen metaphorically as contending perspectives or voices within the lover's own mind. In our own lives, we, like the lover, sometimes fear the voices from the different aspects of our own being—even from our true self—as alien or unwelcome perspectives. By learning to welcome, respect, and treat with dignity the diverse perspectives of the various aspects of our being, we can gain access to consultation in our inner life and dramatically deepen our understanding and accelerate our spiritual growth. The subject of consulting within the self will also be treated more thoroughly in our next book.

Chapter 9

Putting Our Learning into Action—Living a Purposeful Life

The opening question for this book was, *Now that I am here, what should I be doing?* Back in Chapter 3, we had a first "answer progress report" in response to this question. Now, after covering additional ground, it's time to have an augmented answer report.

Answer Progress Report

We have now identified a range of inter-related answers to the title question. The *first answer* is to fulfill the three ultimate purposes of life—to know and love God, to acquire spiritual attributes, and to carry forward an ever-advancing civilization. The *second answer* is about the perspective we need to hold and it has two dimensions: as we work on our own personal approach to achieving the three purposes, we need to see the world as a spiritual growth lab designed by an all-loving Creator Who provides each of us with a never-ending series of tailor-made opportunities to foster our learning and spiritual growth; and we need to expect this tailored curriculum to be characterized by tests and difficulties that we must navigate to achieve our purposes.

These first two answers define the context and larger spiritual drama of all our lives. However, each of us travels a personal path with our own unique set of experiences, circumstances, and capacities that equip us to fulfill the purposes of life in our own unique way; and we each fulfill, somewhat fulfill, or fail to fulfill the three ultimate purposes of life based on our own choices and decisions. To make the best choices and decisions, we need to understand as much as we can about the dynamics of change and spiritual growth we are likely to encounter in life's growth lab. The remaining answers to our title question relate more specifically to managing the *growth dynamics* on the personal path to purpose.

The *third answer* to our question addresses these growth dynamics in terms of the *directional forces* of the spiritual growth lab of life. It has the following five dimensions, each of which was the subject of an earlier chapter of this book:

- The spiritual growth lab of life is calling us toward spiritual reality;

- The spiritual growth lab of life is calling forth our true self;

- The spiritual growth lab of life is calling us to the guided condition;

- The spiritual growth lab of life is calling us toward spiritual growth;

- And the spiritual growth lab of life is calling us toward collaborative rather than adversarial human interactions.

If the spiritual growth lab of life were a river, the *divine currents* are pulling us toward these five destinations. We are free to move against these currents, but they will probably increase our struggle and result in our landing in some worldly destination that deprives us of our spiritual birthright. However, if we are mindful of these divine currents, we can use them to expedite a journey that is difficult enough without adding further resistance. Our objective is to leverage the river's five currents or directional forces to navigate all the way to the ocean of reunion—which is to abide in spiritual reality, our true self, and the guided condition while skillfully achieving spiritual growth through collaborative rather than adversarial human interactions.

Let us consider the *fourth answer* to the question, *Now that I am here, what should I be doing?* This answer also addresses managing the dynamics of the spiritual growth lab of life and it focuses on our overall role and approach. The answer, based on the Watchman Parable, is that the best way to navigate the dynamics of the spiritual growth lab of life toward the fulfillment of our purposes is in the role of a Wall-Seeker rather than a wall-avoider; and we provided relevant definitions to help us understand the general Wall-Seeker role and approach.

> **Wall**, n **1:** an obstacle, impediment, or boundary; **2:** a structure, force, or dynamic that separates one from objects or conditions existing on the other side

> **Seeker**, n **1:** one who is in a state of active search, discovery, or inquiry; **2:** one searching for something more or different; **3**: one who strives to go beyond

> **Wall-seeker,** n **1**: one who views walls as indicators of the existence of something precious waiting unseen, nearby; **2**: one who welcomes walls as mileposts to be scaled on the journey toward growth and greater spiritual awareness; **3**: one who views opposing or challenging forces as divine emissaries and guides; **4**: one who makes decisions and takes action accordingly

Clearly, Wall-Seekers are people who investigate and navigate reality by seeing with a spiritual eye and hearing with a spiritual ear. They focus first on spiritual reality and secondarily on material reality in order to live a purposeful life.

The *fifth answer* to our title question further unfolds the fourth answer by addressing the specific methodology the Wall-Seeker uses to manage the dynamics of life's growth lab. The answer is that our journey will be expedited through the spiritual growth lab toward the three ultimate purposes of life

if we manage the dynamics contained in the following fifteen
Wall-Seeker principles:

The Wall-Seeker Principles of Change and Spiritual Growth

Principle #1: Suffering and loss are inherent in the process of change and spiritual growth.

Principle #2: In order to change and grow spiritually, it helps to follow a sequence of:

- Becoming humble and submissive in response to God's guidance;

- Taking action to engage with others or our self on the issue;

- Making ourselves vulnerable, detaching from life as we know it, and climbing with difficulty toward a higher spiritual dimension;

- Being willing to sacrifice, making a signal act of faith, and trusting in divine guidance.

Principle #3: There is joy somewhere on the other side of the wall.

Principle #4: The "beloved" we seek may look different and/or be in a different place than we had expected.

Principle #5: Several apparently random, unconnected events in one's life may be intensely connected in their meaning to one's life.

Principle #6: There is guiding intention in the universe—things are happening to you that are meant to guide you along a tailored growth path.

Principle #7: There is multiplicity of guiding intention in the universe—things are happening to everyone else that are meant to guide them along tailored growth paths.

Principle #8: There is synchronicity designed into life— things that happen to you to guide you along a growth path may be synchronized and intersect with things that are happening to someone else to guide them along a growth path.

Principle #9: There is multiple intentioned synchronicity designed into life. Synchronized growth path occurrences are happening to all people and our lives are intersecting in highly complex, multi-dimensional patterns in which we are the "lover" for some, the "beloved" for others, and "watchmen" for still others. In turn, others we encounter potentially play all these roles for us.

Principle #10: We should welcome the watchmen in our lives—it is a waste of time and energy to try to determine if they are motivated by love or wrath.

Principle #11: The goal in life is to grow spiritually—to use the watchmen in our lives to quickly identify the walls we need to scale for change and spiritual growth, and then to go over them as rapidly as possible.

Principle #12: The difficulties and suffering we experience in life are intended to lead us away from self-absorption & limitation, and toward reliance on divine assistance & the infinite.

Principle #13: Having both self-compassion and compassion for others deepens understanding.

Principle #14: In resolving issues, collaborative consultation informed by divine assistance results in greater understanding and spiritual growth than does adversarial contention.

Principle #15: The key to aligning *being* and *doing* in our lives is seeing the end in the beginning.

In the remainder of this final chapter, we will put our learning into action by further exploring the five answers to our title question, putting special emphasis on the fifteen Wall-Seeker Principles, and illustrating their use with real-life examples. Names have been changed for all the people in the application examples except for the personal examples we have chosen to identify. In the personal examples, Jean will narrate the ones relating to Bill and Bill the ones relating to Jean.

Using the Fifteen Wall-Seeker Principles for a Purposeful Life

Let us review and further explore the fifteen Wall-Seeker Principles drawn from earlier sections of the book to guide us as we leverage our circumstances to better navigate the spiritual growth lab of life and achieve the three purposes of life.

PRINCIPLE #1:
Suffering and loss are inherent in the process of change and spiritual growth.

Living a purposeful life requires that we think differently from the way our culture teaches us to think, which is that well-being and happiness are largely associated with comfort, entertainment, self-gratification, self-satisfaction, acquiring belongings and assets, and achieving affluence and status in society. While the Wall-Seeker is neither immune to these benefits nor ascetic in approaching life, he or she realizes that these benefits are just alleviations to be used for rapidly refreshing ourselves for the primary purposes of life—the struggle to know and love God, acquire spiritual attributes, and carry forward an ever-advancing civilization. As a result, Wall-Seekers willingly and regularly sacrifice comfort and *proactively* approach suffering and loss.

"This Isn't Comfy, Linda!"

When one of our daughters was taking dance lessons with other six-year-old girls, we would often observe the classes with other parents. One day the girls were working on a new ballet position that required stretching their feet and legs beyond their normal limits. After holding the new position for a few seconds, one of the girls said to the instructor, "This isn't comfy, Linda!" Those of us watching the class did our best to stifle our laughter, but it was a great illustration of the fact that, from childhood on up through adulthood, we do not tend to associate learning and growth with discomfort. In reality, growth begins where the comfort zone ends. Being a skilled navigator through the spiritual growth lab of life requires that we incorporate this fact into our thinking.

Who Knows What Is Good or What Is Bad?

Another way in which living a purposeful life requires us to think differently from the way our culture teaches us to think is in our evaluation of the things that happen to us. If we are committed to the cultural values of well-being that would have us seek comfort, entertainment, and self-gratification, we will view any form of inconvenience, discomfort, adversity, suffering, or loss that enters our lives as misfortune. The Wall-Seeker learns to view such things differently. He or she learns to reject the labels of good or bad. An old Taoist story illustrates the wisdom in this approach.

When an old farmer's stallion won a prize at a country show, his neighbor called on him to congratulate him, but the old farmer said, "Who knows what is good and what is bad?" The next day some thieves came and stole his valuable animal. His neighbor called on him again to commiserate with him, but the old man replied, "Who knows what is good and what is bad?"

A few days later the spirited stallion escaped from the thieves and joined a herd of wild mares, leading them back to the farm. The neighbor called to share the farmer's joy, but the farmer said, "Who knows what is good and what is bad?"

The following day, while trying to break in one of the wild mares, the farmer's son was thrown from the horse and fractured his leg. The neighbor called to share the farmer's sorrow, but the old man's attitude remained the same as before. The following week, the army passed by forcibly conscripting soldiers for a war, but they did not take the farmer's son because he could not walk.

The neighbor thought to himself, "Who knows what is good and what is bad?" and realized that the old farmer was a Taoist sage. [1]

Implicit in this Wall-Seeking perspective is the humble recognition that God knows better than we do what is best for us and that the tailored curriculum he has prepared for us is the optimum path for our spiritual development. Reflecting this perspective is the following prayer excerpt from the Bahá'í Writings.

> Ordain Thou for me, O my God, the good of this world and the world to come, and grant me what will profit me in every world of Thy worlds, for I

> know not what will help or harm me. Thou, in truth,
> art the All-Knowing, the All-Wise. ²

Living a purposeful life requires that we transcend the labels of worldly culture and focus on the growth requirements for the journeying soul.

Going Beyond Rejecting the Labels of What Is Good or Bad

Like the Taoist sage, when we learn to reject the labels of good and bad in relation to what happens in our lives, we are able to focus simply on what is. But embracing purposeful living requires that we go beyond the mere rejection of these labels and *proactively* use the events in our lives to *accelerate* our spiritual growth and capacity to serve. We do so by proactively asking Wall-Seeking questions such as: What beloved am I seeking or wanting? What watchmen forces am I experiencing? What obstacles or walls do I need to go over to reach my goal? To which of the three life purposes does this situation apply? And what virtues do I need to develop to achieve my goal and beloved?

Embracing the Value of Suffering

Another way in which a purposeful life requires that we think differently has to do with our attitude toward suffering. Our culture teaches us to react to the suffering of our acquaintances with the unspoken question, "Where did they go wrong?" This attitude carries the assumption that suffering only happens as a result of foolish behavior. The truth is that life is meant to entail regular struggle; if it were constantly smooth and comfortable, growth would not occur. The Watchman Parable teaches us that suffering is an integral part of life and is necessary for our spiritual development.

Other Holy Writings confirm this truth. The Hindu Writings say:

> Welcome to thy wrath and to thy glow!

Our welcome be to thy flame!
Let thy missiles burn our enemies,
Be our purifier, be gracious to us! [3]

The Muslim Writings advise us to be patient in response to suffering.

> You who believe, seek help through patience and prayer; God stands alongside the patient!...We will test you with a bit of fear and hunger, and a shortage of wealth and souls and produce. Proclaim such to patient people who say, whenever disaster strikes them, "We are God's, and are returning to Him!" Such will be granted their prayers by their Lord as well as mercy. Those are guided! [4]

The Bahá'í Writings tell us that suffering reconnects us to our Creator and reminds us of our spiritual nature.

> While a man is happy he may forget his God; but when grief comes and sorrows overwhelm him, then will he remember his Father who is in Heaven, and who is able to deliver him from his humiliations. [5]

These Writings also indicate that suffering helps us fulfill the purposes of life by fostering the development of spiritual attributes.

> Tests are benefits from God, for which we should thank Him. Grief and sorrow do not come to us by chance, they are sent to us by the Divine Mercy for our own perfecting....
>
> Men who suffer not, attain no perfection. The plant most pruned by the gardeners is that one which, when the summer comes, will have the most beautiful blossoms and the most abundant fruit.

The labourer cuts up the earth with his plough, and from that earth comes the rich and plentiful harvest. The more a man is chastened, the greater is the harvest of spiritual virtues shown forth by him.[6]

Addressing Suffering and Loss through Action

Suffering and loss can take many forms, some of them tremendously intense. They may involve the loss of a loved one, a serious illness, or the loss of a physical function; or they could entail being frustrated about the condition of our life, the loss of a friendship, leaving behind a favored phase of life, a professional failure, the loss of an opportunity or dream, the undercutting of our self-worth, or other forms of disappointment, emotional stress, and abuse.

While living a purposeful life entails embracing the *value* of suffering, it does not involve *wallowing* in it. Like the lover in the parable who ultimately heads for the marketplace, interacts with watchmen, and scales the wall, Wall-Seekers *do* something about suffering—they address suffering and loss through collaborative interactions with others to help reveal the wall separating them from joy and the beloved. And then they scale the wall.

A friend of ours lost her beloved son to a terminal illness when he was only ten years old. The suffering and loss she experienced was crushing; but she soon began reflecting about what she could do to carry forward her son's spirit and aspiration in the world. Remembering that saving the earth's environment had been a theme close to his heart, she began conferring with others and then started a non-profit organization that creates, publishes, and distributes learning materials about maintaining a green planet to school systems for children to use in the classroom. Her suffering led her to take action to scale a wall. On the other side of that wall, she discovered a beloved which was a passion for creating and running a business that simultaneously honors her son's memory and contributes to the advancement of civilization.

The Risk of Being Overwhelmed by Suffering

Wall-Seekers can sometimes be overwhelmed by suffering, but they have developed the ability to call themselves back from the brink by remembering the three ultimate purposes of life: to know and love God, to acquire spiritual attributes, and to carry forward an ever-advancing civilization. They realize that, while all three of these purposes require suffering if we are to fulfill them, we are being supported in our journey by the five directional forces of the spiritual growth lab of life, which are calling forth our true self and calling us to spiritual reality, the guided condition, spiritual growth, and collaborative interactions. Reminding ourselves of these five great supportive forces and the tailored spiritual growth curriculum the Creator has laid out before each of us, helps inspire us to think like the anonymous person who said:

> Sometimes I go about pitying myself, and all the time
> I am being carried on great winds across the sky.[7]

The Holy Writings also assure us of the value of suffering. The Muslim Writings say:

> The believer who participates in human life, exposing himself to its torments and suffering, is worth more than the one who distances himself from its suffering.[8]

And the Bahá'í Writings say:

> O SON OF MAN!
> My calamity is My providence, outwardly it is fire and vengeance, but inwardly it is light and mercy. Hasten thereunto that thou mayest become an eternal light and an immortal spirit. This is My command unto thee, do thou observe it.[9]

These same Writings assure us that suffering helps us effectively navigate to the next world.

> O thou servant of God! Do not grieve at the afflictions and calamities that have befallen thee. All calamities and afflictions have been created for man so that he may spurn this mortal world -- a world to which he is much attached. When he experienceth severe trials and hardships, then his nature will recoil and he will desire the eternal realm -- a realm which is sanctified from all afflictions and calamities. Such is the case with the man who is wise. He shall never drink from a cup which is at the end distasteful, but, on the contrary, he will seek the cup of pure and limpid water. He will not taste of the honey that is mixed with poison. [10]

Wall-Seekers Keep Their Thinking on Track

Living a purposeful life means that we keep our thinking on track as we navigate through suffering and loss by:

- Expecting and accepting discomfort as the sidecar to growth;
- Rejecting the labels of good or bad to define what happens;
- Embracing the value of suffering;
- Addressing suffering and loss through action;
- Calling ourselves back from the brink of being overwhelmed by suffering.

Keeping our thinking on track in these ways is all-important. In the Judaic Writings, we are told, "Keep thy heart with all diligence; for out of it are the issues of life." [11] Putting this in common parlance, one could say, "Be careful about your thinking; your thinking shapes your life."

In the end, Wall-Seekers keep their thinking on track by embracing the mystical role that suffering plays in the soul's journey. In addition, they realize that, in terms of tests, difficulties, and suffering, God knows *what* we will go through in life, but we choose *how* we will go through it.

PRINCIPLE #2:
In order to change and grow spiritually, it helps to follow a sequence of:

1. Becoming humble and submissive in response to God's guidance;

2. Taking action to engage with others or our self on the issue;

3. Making ourselves vulnerable, detaching from life as we know it, and climbing with difficulty toward a higher spiritual dimension;

4. Being willing to sacrifice, making a signal act of faith, and trusting in divine guidance.

While the change and spiritual growth process is often triggered by some form of suffering or loss, Wall-Seeking Principle #2 describes how we *become ripe* for change and spiritual growth. This ripening process ideally begins with becoming humble and submissive in response to God's guidance.

Becoming Humble & Submissive in Response to God's Guidance

A potential spiritual benefit of suffering is that it can dilate the heart by making us humbly aware of our fragility and dependence on our Creator. We say "potential" spiritual benefit because, in the absence of humility and submission, suffering can make us angry at God, ourselves, or others; it can make us bitter and resentful; and it can make us envious of others who do not seem to suffer. When humility is present, however, suffering makes us aware that we have an opportunity to grow and that we need to submissively ask for God's assistance.

Unlike the lover in the Watchman Parable, we want to become humble and submissive from the beginning of the suffering rather than resisting or warring against the watchmen. When we let our hearts lament, the realization of our weakness makes us humble; and awareness of being in the grip of God's plan for us makes us submissive. We become meek.

Meekness does not imply a lack of courage; rather it implies enduring with patience and without resentment, being mild and gentle, being submissive, moderate, and humble. While meekness is not highly valued in materialistic cultures where "personality" is given precedence, the world's Holy Writings place high value on it as a component of spiritual advancement for both the individual and society. Speaking of the educational influence of the Messengers or Manifestations of God on humanity, the Bahá'í Writings say:

> Man is selfish; They [the Messengers of God] sever him from self and desire. Man is haughty; They make him meek, humble and friendly. He is earthly; They make him heavenly. Men are material; the Manifestations [Messengers] transform them into semblance divine. [12]

The Muslim Writings give precedence to meekness as a qualification for leadership.

> We wished to favor those who were weak in the land and make them leaders and heirs. [13]

And the Christian Writings make meekness central to the advancement of civilization.

Blessed are the meek, for they shall inherit the earth. [14]

Clearly, both individual spiritual growth and carrying forward an ever-advancing civilization are expedited by humility, submission, and meekness because these attributes have a *purifying* influence on the heart and foster behavior that is in line with God's guidance and teachings.

Taking Action to Engage with Others or Our Self on the Issue

Living a purposeful life requires action. Having been influenced by suffering and loss and an increase in humility and submissiveness, the Wall-Seeker takes *action* for change and spiritual growth. The word "seeker" means to go to, to go in search of, to look for, to try to discover, to try to acquire or gain, to make an attempt, and to try. It is the opposite of a passive, static, and lethargic existence. The idea that spiritual attainment requires action is not new. As previously referenced, the Christian Writings say:

> Ask, and it shall be given you; seek, and ye shall find; knock, and it shall be opened unto you: For every one that asketh receiveth; and he that seeketh findeth; and to him that knocketh it shall be opened. [15]

Accordingly, the Wall-Seeker responds to the watchmen in her or his life by collaboratively interacting with them as a means of actively seeking the wall that needs to be scaled. As the Wall-Seeker scales the wall, he or she is preparing for the action of throwing himself or herself into the darkness of the unknown in order to meet the beloved. This action may spring from collaborative consultation within the individual or in a group, but it involves full engagement with the issue at hand.

The Example of Joe—Seeing Opportunity in Crisis by Engaging with Self & Others

A client of ours named Joe, who was becoming very skilled in living a purposeful life, demonstrated remarkable Wall-Seeking behavior. He was fifty years old, had worked for ten years for the same organization, and one day was called into a meeting with his boss and his boss' boss. It didn't take long in the conversation for Joe to realize they were about to terminate his employment. As they talked, he felt a wave of panic, sadness, and loss pass over him; but then, realizing this was part of his curriculum in the spiritual growth lab of life, he felt humble and submissive to the will and guidance of God.

Once he did this, he could concentrate more clearly on what the watchmen (his bosses) were saying to him. The gist of what they were saying was that the organization had to deploy resources in new areas and that, while Joe's skills in certain areas would be sorely missed, his position was being eliminated at the end of thirty days to free up resources. As they talked, Joe began thinking about what the wall was that he needed to scale. In that same spirit of inquiry, he decided to engage collaboratively with the watchmen; he asked his bosses to clarify the skill areas that they would miss in his absence.

After the meeting, Joe fought off feelings of panic, embarrassment, and shame about "being fired." He forced himself to sit alone and consult with himself about what the wall was. For some years, he had flirted with the idea of self-employment as a consultant but always danced away from the idea for reasons of financial security. Now, he sensed this was the wall beckoning him. That night, Joe collaboratively consulted with his wife about the situation. She was supportive and suggested that his bosses had clearly outlined the skill sets they would miss in his absence, and that these skills could be the core of his consulting offering.

To make a longer story shorter, after two weeks of collaboratively consulting with other people, Joe scheduled another meeting with his bosses, told them he was starting a consulting business, and offered to provide the selected services they needed from him as a consultant. They agreed to become his first client organization.

The launch of Joe's business was very challenging in many ways, but Joe was successful and the beloved he discovered on the other side of the wall was the dramatically increased freedom he had in this new arena to be of service to others and fulfill the three ultimate purposes of life in his own unique way.

Taking Action = Moving Away from and Moving Toward

Living a purposeful life requires that, like Joe, we resist the lethargy and passivity that contemporary culture induces, and take action to engage with ourselves and others on the issue before us. Actively stepping forward always involves moving away from something and toward something else. When taking action, what do Wall-Seekers move away from and toward? They *move away* from the mindless constructs of cultural learning they have inherited that invigorate our lower nature and keep us from growing. In Joe's case, he moved away from panic, sadness, and the embarrassment of "being fired." Wall-Seekers *move toward* the testing ground and spiritual growth lab of life that calls forth our true self and calls us toward spiritual reality, the guided condition, spiritual growth, and collaborative consultation. In Joe's case, as soon as the pattern of distress, watchmen, and wall became apparent, he immediately embraced humility and submission and then started engaging with himself and others (including the watchmen) in a collaborative fashion to address the issue, identify the wall, and begin scaling it.

Procrastination vs. Action

Because change requires new, unfamiliar, and uncomfortable ways of thinking and doing, there is a tendency to procrastinate and avoid it, like the lover in the Watchman Parable, until the discomfort and suffering reach unbearable proportions. Wall-Seekers embrace the discomfort and suffering *early* in order to reach the beloved sooner and fulfill rather than squander the purpose of this brief time on earth. The choice between acquiescing in the status quo or committing to active change and spiritual growth is constantly with each one of us. The nature of the issue and outcome are well described in a traditional Native American story:

> A young Indian boy went to the village shaman. The boy was troubled and said to the elder, "Help me. There is a war inside my heart. Part of me wants to travel east, and another part wants to travel west. What do I do?" The old man nodded. The boy's problem was a familiar one. "Within each man," the shaman said, "lives two dogs. Both dogs are strong and fight for the man's heart; one to go east, and one to go west. The man chooses which dog will win by deciding which dog he will feed."[16]

Wall-Seekers choose to feed the dog that moves toward spiritual growth.

Making Ourselves Vulnerable

Successfully changing and growing also requires that we make ourselves vulnerable. To become "vulnerable" means to have the courage to step into what is unfamiliar or uncomfortable and to open oneself to the possibility of receiving a physical or emotional wound. If I want to learn a new dive off the diving board, for example, I must step into unfamiliar terrain and open myself to the possibility of experiencing a painful belly flop as well as the laughter from those who may witness it. If we do not make ourselves vulnerable, the guards and defenses we normally maintain (e.g. acting superior, blaming others, practicing denial, or suppressing painful thoughts) will keep us in the familiar terrain of the status quo and prevent us from gaining new understanding and spiritual attributes.

Ira was a successful trial attorney who made his living winning adversarial arguments in the courtroom. However, his marriage was in trouble because he habitually used these same skills to address issues and disagreements with his wife. For Ira, making himself vulnerable entailed resisting his adversarial instincts and instead saying to his wife, "Tell me more about what's troubling you" and "How can we make it better?" Ira learned these skills, but was surprised at how much courage and concentration it required of him to break out of the status quo and change his habit.

In the Watchman Parable, the lover is not making himself vulnerable when he is running in fear from the watchmen—he is maintaining his guards and defenses. It is only when he stops running at the garden wall and begins to *face* his situation that he makes himself vulnerable by beginning to scale the wall.

The Example of Mary—Detaching from Life as We Know It

Mary had been engaged to Paul for two months and, on the surface, her life was perfect. She had an excellent job, Paul was already wildly successful in his career, their two sets of friends seemed to like and get along with each other, their two families had approved the relationship, and Paul was handsome and fun to be with. They both wanted children and seemed to have similar values. However, as the weeks ticked by, Mary could feel the relationship getting more and more toxic. Paul was increasingly controlling, demeaning, and abrasive to her in their private moments, and she found herself feeling lonely in his presence. At one level, Mary realized she needed to break the engagement and get out of the relationship because she longed for an authentic and spiritually fulfilling relationship. But at another level, her heart was attached to the "perfect appearance" of the relationship from a social perspective. It appeared to have all the right ingredients in terms of worldly success and happiness. She could feel the "cultural momentum" pushing her and Paul toward marriage.

Attachment to things worldly culture teaches us to value—such as status, possessions, fun, power, beauty, comfort, titles, luxurious lifestyles, and self-gratification—can distract us from spiritual reality and true Wall-Seeking. If we use Wall-Seeking to achieve a *worldly* rather than *spiritual* beloved, we will surely be disappointed. We must detach from the worldly life that feeds our lower nature because it will lead us away from our spiritual path toward false beloveds that will leave us empty.

The Holy Writings warn us in this regard. The Jewish Writings say:

> This world is like a vestibule before the World to Come; prepare yourself in the vestibule that you may enter the hall. [17]

The Christian Writings say:

> Do not lay up for yourselves treasures on earth, where moth and rust consume and where thieves break in and steal, but lay up for yourselves treasure in heaven, where neither moth nor rust consumes and where thieves do not break in and steal. For where your treasure is, there will your heart be also. [18]

The Islamic Writings say:

> Wealth and sons are the adornment of the present world; but the abiding things, the deeds of righteousness, are better with God in reward, and better in hope. [19]

And the Bahá'í Writings say:

> The world is but a show, vain and empty, a mere nothing, bearing the semblance of reality. Set not your affections upon it. Break not the bond that uniteth you with your Creator, and be not of those that have erred and strayed from His ways. Verily I say, the world is like the vapor in a desert, which the thirsty dreameth to be water and striveth after it with all his might, until when he cometh unto it,

he findeth it to be mere illusion. It may, moreover, be likened unto the lifeless image of the beloved whom the lover hath sought and found, in the end, after long search and to his utmost regret, to be such as cannot "fatten nor appease his hunger."[20]

As a result of suffering and loss, becoming humble and submissive, taking action to address the issue, and becoming vulnerable, Wall-Seekers' affections are pried loose from "the world" and they detach from life as they have known it. Like the lover in the Watchman Parable, the loosening of their grip on "the world" enables them to look upward to their Creator, see the garden wall, and commit to the spiritual regimen required to scale it.

In the end, this is just what Mary did. By detaching from the "beautiful picture" her relationship with Paul represented socially, she freed herself to scale the wall of ending the toxic relationship and accepting the social embarrassment that came with canceling the engagement. One year later, she discovered a new marriage partner with whom she had both a physical and a true spiritual bond. She had honored the truth that "The pathway of life is the road which leads to divine knowledge and attainment."[21]

Climbing with Difficulty toward a Higher Spiritual Dimension

To climb toward a higher spiritual dimension means to make an advance in terms of knowing and loving God, acquiring spiritual attributes, or contributing to an ever-advancing civilization—the three ultimate purposes of life. The lover in the Watchman Parable began this process unwittingly and symbolically by starting to scale the garden wall—he began moving in a vertical or spiritual dimension instead of the horizontal or purely worldly dimension which had him locked into seeing the watchmen as adversaries. He began climbing toward his Creator, acquiring new spiritual attributes such as courage, dauntlessness, and sacrifice, and stopped contending with the watchmen. In so doing, his perspective was *reframed* in such a way that he began addressing his issue in terms of the life of the spirit rather than just the life of the flesh. He began to see and act on new dimensions of meaning in the spiritual realm. We do this when we *proactively* reframe our worldly dilemmas in the context of Wall-Seeking and ask ourselves questions such as:

- What are the purposes of life and how does this situation relate to them?
- What is trying to happen here?
- Where in my life are watchmen forces cornering me?
- What are the watchmen forces driving me toward?
- What is the wall I need to scale?
- What is the beloved I am seeking?
- What is the greater truth about this situation?

Such questions help us discover walls and climb toward higher spiritual dimensions. This kind of questioning and climbing helped Mary end her engagement and toxic relationship. This kind of questioning and climbing led Joe to start his own business and claim his first client. And the common denominator of all of our efforts to climb toward a higher spiritual dimension is that we do it with difficulty. How could it be otherwise when spiritual growth is involved?

Being Willing to Sacrifice

Nearness to God requires that we sacrifice our lower nature for our higher nature and the less important for the more important. Whereas climbing with difficulty toward a higher spiritual dimension may involve recognizing the wall and beginning to scale it, being willing to sacrifice involves scaling the entire wall despite whatever difficulties are involved—including letting go of whatever is inhibiting our journey. This may entail such things as giving up a tightly-held position in an argument, acknowledging a mistake or shortcoming, abandoning comfort and security to go the extra mile for someone or oneself, or letting go of a dream or goal held close to the heart. In the case of Mary, sacrifice meant giving up "the perfect" relationship and embracing aloneness and the search for a new beloved. For Joe, sacrifice meant giving up his need for financial security and embracing the risks and the adventure in going his own way. In essence, sacrifice involves letting go of our way for the more divinely guided way. The Bahá'í Writings say:

> Ask not of Me that which We desire not for thee, then be content with what We have ordained for thy sake, for this is that which profiteth thee, if therewith thou dost content thyself. [22]

These same Writings also say:

> "...to make a sacrifice is to receive a gift..." [23]

Making a Signal Act of Faith

Whereas scaling one side of a wall entails sacrifice, throwing oneself over the wall into the darkness on the other side entails a signal act of faith. It involves trusting in God or something beyond one's self to break one's fall—just as the lover did in the Watchman Parable.

A "signal" act is outstanding, noticeable, and distinguished from the ordinary in terms of one's life. For one individual, *the sacrifice* could be something as simple (but not easy) as saying to a loved one in the heat of argument, "I'm sorry!" *The signal act of faith* could be something as simple (but not easy) as saying, "What's going on with me that I behaved in this way?" While the sacrifice is *letting go* of something closely held, the signal act of faith is *moving forward* in some way into dark terrain.

In the case of Joe, the sacrifice was giving up his need for financial security, and the signal act of faith was launching and carrying through on the new business his heart was calling him toward. In Mary's case, the sacrifice was letting go of a "socially perfect" relationship, and the signal act of faith was not settling for a flawed relationship and moving forward alone despite the risks of social censure and never finding a mate. In both of these cases, something outstanding, noticeable, and distinguished from the ordinary in terms of faith has occurred that moves the person's life forward.

Ultimately, the signal act of faith is a signal to ourselves and our Creator that true spiritual growth has occurred. We give proof that we have passed a test of faith.

Trusting in Divine Guidance

The signal act of faith must be *sustained* by trust in divine guidance. There is a span of time after the lover throws himself into the darkness but before he lands on the ground in the garden and sees the beloved. In our own lives, this span of time may be hours, days, weeks, months, or even years depending on the nature of the wall and the growth required of us in order to find the beloved. During this time—whether short or long—the Wall-Seeker must trust in divine guidance. The Creator wants us to learn the truth that:

> No man that seeketh Us will We ever disappoint,
> neither shall he that hath set his face toward Us be
> denied access unto Our court. [24]

Even if our trust in divine guidance is alloyed with fear, the trust must win out. As Mark Twain said, "Courage is resistance to fear, mastery of fear, not absence of fear." [25] By trusting in divine guidance over time, the Wall-Seeker is learning to honor through action the following admonitions of the Creator:

> Be thou content with Me and seek no other helper.
> For none but Me can ever suffice thee. [26]

And:

> Turn thy face unto Mine and renounce all save Me;
> for My sovereignty endureth and My dominion

perisheth not. If thou seekest another than Me, yea, if thou searchest the universe for evermore, thy quest will be in vain.[27]

PRINCIPLE #3:
There is joy somewhere on the other side of the wall.

One of the mysteries of the life of the spirit is that all the struggle and suffering involved in determinedly living a purposeful life leads to joy. When we content ourselves with striving in our own personal way to achieve the three ultimate life purposes that have been ordained for us, we experience joy and peace. Whether we are given poverty, wealth, or something in between, the test is to see if we grow closer to our Creator, develop spiritual attributes, and contribute to the advancement of civilization, or miss the whole point of being here. Lasting joy comes only from adhering to divine guidance and our God-given purposes.

The Holy Writings confirm this principle. The Hindu writings say:

> The Infinite is the source of joy. There is no joy in the finite. Only in the Infinite is there joy. Ask to know the Infinite.[28]

The Judaic Writings say:

> Thou dost show me the path of life;
> in thy presence there is fullness of joy,
> in thy right hand are pleasures for evermore.[29]

The Christian Writings say:

> The kingdom of God is not food and drink but righteousness and peace and joy in the Holy Spirit.[30]

The Muslim Writings say:

> No person knows what delights of the eye are
> kept hidden for them—as a reward for their good
> deeds. [31]

And the Bahá'í Writings say:

> If thou art desiring divine joy, free thyself from the
> bands of attachment.[32]

And:

> True happiness depends on spiritual good and
> having the heart ever open to receive the Divine
> Bounty. [33]

It is apparent that for a Wall-Seeker to experience joy beyond
the wall, she or he must first free the heart from impeding worldly
attachments and then open it to the influence of its Creator. What
else causes the lover's spiritual evolution in the parable from a
wall-avoider to a Wall-Seeker, and from a miserable soul to a joyful
soul? Suffering plays a role in this process because the dilation of
heart caused by suffering helps the heart open and vibrate to the
Divine Bounty like a tuning fork. In the Watchman Parable, this
joy-inducing process is described as one requiring a "heart-surrendered lover." [34]

PRINCIPLE #4:

*The "beloved" we seek may look different
and/or be in a different place than we had
expected.*

One of the best known and loved short stories of O. Henry is
"The Gift of the Magi." It is the story of Jim and Della, a young
married couple who are deeply in love and frightfully poor; each

is distressed about being unable to afford a Christmas gift for the other that will adequately convey their love. Each of them has a single, prized possession. Jim has a beautiful gold pocket watch that has been passed down to him from his father and grandfather. Della has her long, beautiful hair. After much agonizing, each of them independently and privately has a brilliant inspiration. Jim decides to sell his prized watch in order to buy an elegant set of decorative combs for Della's beautiful hair. Della decides to sell her prized hair in order to buy a platinum chain that will attach to Jim's cherished watch. When they exchange their gifts, the moment is filled with great irony, poignancy, and meaning.

From the Wall-Seeking perspective, the "perfect gift"—the beloved each received—turned out to be *different than was expected*. Ironically, the gift each gave was the intended companion piece to the prized possession the other had sacrificed for love. Both Della and Jim had tried to convey a "beloved" to the other that was *material* in nature; but what actually occurred was that each conveyed a "beloved" that was *spiritual* in nature. Each was able to let go of what he or she most prized materially in order to make the other one happy, and spiritual growth occurred as a result of these sacrifices. Consequently, the actual beloveds (gifts) had far more spiritual power and significance than either lover could have expected. These are also characteristics of Wall-Seeking in our personal lives because when *true beloveds* appear, they often have *unexpected* dimensions that cause us to stretch and grow *spiritually*.

The Nature of True Beloveds

Often we find ourselves seeking a beloved that will simply relieve our suffering. We may seek a better job, higher income, or a friend to spend time with. In this sense, we are thinking of the beloved as something one-dimensional in nature. When the beloved actually appears, it is typically two-, three-, or four-dimensional in nature.

Multi-Dimensional Impacts

For example, in the Watchman Parable, the lover simply sought the beloved woman who he believed would relieve his longing and suffering. When the beloved actually appeared, it included the woman, but also enhanced spiritual awareness and relationship with his Creator and the watchmen. Similarly, in "The Gift of the Magi," Della and Jim were simply trying to overcome their inability to afford a precious material gift for each other. What actually appeared in their respective beloveds included the material gifts, but also the spiritual gifts of sensitivity, love, devotion, detachment, self-effacement, and sacrifice for each other. Among the beloveds we may seek, *true beloveds have a multi-dimensional impact on our lives.*

Some years ago, we coached a hard-driving executive who wanted to find a significant other. She was convinced she had not yet met the man who was right for her. This was the unknown beloved she sought. Together we discovered that the wall she needed to scale was the softening of her heart. As she learned to scale this wall and throw herself over it into the darkness of becoming more vulnerable and compassionate, she experienced a healthy new relationship with herself, and dramatic improvement in a few troubled relationships with professional colleagues. She recognized that these changes were aspects of the beloved she sought. Subsequently, she fell in love with, and later married, a man who was already in her network of friends, but with whom there had never previously been a romantic spark. Not only did her beloved, in all its dimensions, look different and show up in a different place than she expected, but it had more dimensions than she expected—it involved improved relationships with herself and work colleagues as well. In addition, her "beloved" moved her forward spiritually.

Milestone Beloveds & Destination Beloveds

During the period we were writing this book, Jean went through a slowly evolving and extremely difficult health crisis. The health problem manifested itself over eight years in a series of twenty-three, seven- to fourteen-day hospital stays during which she would be in extreme pain and heavily medicated. Each time Jean slowly got better, received a new set of medications and dietary recommendations and left the hospital, only to return again sooner than the last time with renewed symptoms. The doctors were not sure what to do, and meanwhile her weight kept dropping. Our life patterns, work schedules, and emotions were devastated.

The beloved that we were seeking was Jean's good health. However, in this kind of a slowly-evolving life situation, there are often many walls that need to be scaled and many beloveds that show up during the process of trying to recover and heal. We call the sequence of beloveds that appear in such a long, slowly unfolding Wall-Seeking episode "milestone beloveds," and they often lead to a "destination beloved" such as good health. Milestone beloveds tend to renew us and keep us going toward destination beloveds; and they seem designed by God to protect us from despair.

At one of our lowest points during this health crisis, Jean was at home having recovered from one hospital stay, and we were both anxiously wondering when the next would occur. Neither of us knew where to turn and our lives seemed to be losing their meaning. Preparing for dinner, Jean pulled a cookbook off of the bookshelf above her desk in the kitchen, and two small strips of paper fluttered down onto her desktop. She picked them up, and both of them had the same scriptural quote on them.

> **Blessed are the steadfastly enduring, they that are patient under ills and hardships, who lament not over anything that befalleth them, and who tread the path of resignation...**[35]

Neither of us had any memory of seeing these two strips of paper before and could not imagine how they got lodged between cookbooks on Jean's bookshelf. Nevertheless, there they were—one strip for each of us—with the same scriptural quote that exactly addressed our concerns over where to turn and what meaning this relentless suffering contained. As we read and reread the quotation together and discussed how the strips of paper had appeared, we realized that this was *a milestone beloved*. It was not the *destination beloved* of good health, but it was a much needed message to our hearts and spirits about how we needed to go through these difficult tests. The experience of this milestone beloved protected us from despair and put our thinking back on track. In all of our lives, milestone beloveds renew us in our longer Wall-Seeking journeys toward destination beloveds—and they usually look different and are in different places than we may expect.

The destination beloved of good health for Jean ultimately appeared in a most remarkable way. At the end of this eight-year journey of distress, the two of us left our home in Minnesota for a multi-day national conference in Chicago, and, one night, Jean had an attack of her symptoms that nearly sent us to the hospital; however, the symptoms subsided about 3:00 a.m. We slept later that morning and got to the conference late, feeling depleted, humble, and fragile, during the morning coffee break between conference sessions.

We immediately encountered one of our acquaintances, a physician from the east coast, who asked us why we were arriving so late. We explained Jean's symptoms from the night before. He asked Jean a lengthy battery of questions and then told us he had earlier worked with the two doctors who had been treating Jean. We discovered that his specialty was in the exact area of Jean's condition, and, after assessing her situation, he told us he believed there was a dietary component of Jean's condition that was unaddressed. He told us to make an appointment when we returned home with a physician in the same practice as the two doctors who were already treating Jean, because this physician was a well-known authority on treating conditions like Jean's through diet.

A few weeks later, when we were able to see this doctor, she prescribed a radical change to Jean's diet that virtually eliminated her problems within two days. Now, in the five years after that doctor visit, Jean has not been in a hospital once. The destination beloved, this woman doctor who returned Jean to good health, practiced only a few miles from our home; but we had to travel to Chicago to confer with a wise, compassionate East Coast physician to find her. When the beloved appeared, we discovered more than just good health for Jean; we experienced a deeper devotion to and reliance on our Creator, which is always the ultimate destination beloved.

PRINCIPLE #5:

Several apparently random, unconnected events in one's life may be intensely connected in their meaning to one's life.

In the Watchman Parable, this principle is demonstrated by the sequence of apparently *unconnected* personal decisions and watchmen events that actually form a series of highly relevant and *connected* events culminating in added meaning to the lover's life. We all experience days when we have a specific list of priorities and goals in mind and the day turns out totally different from the way we had intended. On such days, it seems that life has control of us rather than us having control of life. The parable seems to be telling us that, looked at with a spiritual eye, such days may be highly relevant to the meaning of our lives even though we may not recognize it at the time; and our original intentions may be getting fulfilled in an unanticipated and more spiritually significant way. Rather than resisting this dynamic of the spiritual growth lab of life, the Wall-Seeker attempts to maintain a fine balance between *intending to grow* and *going with the flow*.

This dynamic shows up in all of our lives in small and large ways if we are looking for it. Early in Bill's career, before he became a consultant and life coach, he was trying to figure out what profession he should be in to better fulfill his potential and contribute to the advancement of society; however, he had been so busy with his current job and family commitments that he was having trouble finding solitary time to integrate his developing thoughts into a plan of action.

One day, Bill was traveling home with an associate from a

week-long business trip. He and his companion reached the airport, checked in for the flight, and then went to the gate area to wait for boarding. The plan was to spend the time together on the flight discussing work projects.

When it was almost time to board the flight, Bill looked at his ticket and realized he had no seat assignment. When he approached the gate agent, there was only one seat left on the plane; it was not next to his business associate. Bill was about to complain, but caught himself and decided to go with the flow. The one remaining seat turned out to be a solitary one, just behind the pilot's door, with a window view.

Sitting down in the seat and wondering how he would spend his time on the flight, Bill's eyes focused on the airline magazine in the rack in front of him with a headline reading, "The Top Careers in the Next Decade." Immediately, he thought of his stalled search for a new profession. As it turned out, this solitary, reflective space with a window at thirty thousand feet enabled Bill to clarify, create a plan for, and begin moving forward on the next chapter of his professional life. It all arose from several small and apparently unconnected events in his life—checking in and not noticing the absence of a seat assignment, going to the waiting area and sitting for a half-hour before checking his seat assignment, going to the gate agent at exactly the right moment to get the last seat on the plane, seeing the airline magazine with the "Careers" headline, and having that isolated seat provide all the properties to help foster the reflection and integration time he needed. One could say these events were just accidental. However, using a Wall-Seeking perspective, Bill realized these small events were intensely relevant and deeply connected in their meaning to his life.

Being aware that the growth lab of life is continually presenting us with opportunities for new learning and purposeful decision-making helps Wall-Seekers notice them when they start unfolding. It requires a combination of *intending to grow* and *going with the flow* in order to use the events to achieve the deeper understanding and spiritual growth they can foster.

PRINCIPLE #6:

*There is guiding intention in the universe—
things are happening to you that are meant to
guide you along a tailored growth path.*

At every moment of our lives, each of us is positioned some-where on a doubt/faith continuum that runs from "Life is totally random and without meaning" on one end to "Life is totally infused with divine intention and meaning" on the other end. Wall-Seeking involves committing to the process of managing the ups and downs of life from the faith end of the continuum by accepting the principle that there is guiding intention in the universe—things are happening to me that are meant to guide me along a tailored growth path.

In the Watchman Parable, this principle is demonstrated by the fact that the Watchmen, who seem to the lover to be randomly driv-ing him *off course* in terms of his goal, are actually driving him *on course* in terms of his tailored spiritual growth path. What appears to be disruption and obstruction is actually compassionate guidance. It *is not clear* what the watchmen's individual intentions are, but it *is clear* that the Hand of Providence is crafting a tailored spiritual growth program for the lover. The parable seems to convey that in each of our personal lives, much of what appears to be random and coincidental is really designed and intentional.

Other Holy Writings also convey this truth. The Judaic Writings say:

> The heavens are telling the glory of God;
> and the firmament proclaims his handiwork.
> Day to day pours forth speech,
> and night to night declares knowledge.
> There is no speech, nor are there words,
> neither is their voice heard;
> yet their voice goes out through all the earth,

and their words to the end of the world.[36]

The Christian Writings declare:

> For what can be known about God is plain to (all), because God has showed it to them. Ever since the creation of the world his invisible nature, namely, his eternal power and deity, has been clearly perceived in the things that have been made. So they are without excuse. [37]

The Islamic Writings convey:

> We shall show then Our signs on the horizons and within themselves until it becomes clear to them that it is the Truth. [38]

And the Bahá'í Writings state:

> Out of the wastes of nothingness, with the clay of My command I made thee to appear, and have ordained for thy training every atom in existence and the essence of all created things. [39]

Given how random life often appears, it is difficult to get our arms around the concept that God has ordained for our "…training every atom in existence and the essence of all created things." The implication seems to be that every person, thing, event, thought, and moment we encounter are potentially part of this divinely-intended training process if we properly submit ourselves to it.

Most of us only recognize this pattern in our lives looking in the rear-view mirror. We may remember a time of struggle when resistive forces guided us to a better place or kept us safe when the outcome could have been disastrous. The Wall-Seeker strives to see this pattern not in the rear-view mirror, but through the windshield as it approaches. To proactively see this larger pattern in life requires that we develop our inner spiritual eye rather than just rely on our outer worldly eye. The challenge of perception can be likened to a crop circle. When we are up close to the corn field, the corn stalks seem to have been flattened randomly, but from a proper elevation the flattened stalks are creating recurring shapes and patterns. Our worldly eye is so close to life that the material panorama before us appears to be random and without ultimate meaning. Our inner or spiritual eye, however, has the capacity and elevated perspective to see the recurring pattern of divine intention, guidance along our tailored spiritual growth path, and ultimate meaning. It is this eye that helps us live in the guided condition.

The Example of James—Experiencing Tailored Growth Path Guidance

One of our clients experienced tailored growth path guidance that re-confirmed him on a path of growth and faith when he was weighed down with weariness and doubt. James functioned well socially and at work, but went blank when it came to identifying his feelings or emotions. In reviewing his life history, he reported that his father had been very harsh with him and would criticize and humiliate him if he cried or was exuberant. James tended to minimize his experience by saying that his upbringing was probably pretty much like all boys' upbringings; and, like other boys, he simply did not have the capacity to experience and express feelings well. He suspected he was being self-indulgent in even talking about it.

After a month-long lapse in his inner work, James returned with new insight and determination. He said that recently he and his sister had been going through their deceased parents' belongings and found a magazine article their mother had saved. It had been written thirty years earlier by a psychologist who explained the impact on men of harsh upbringings in which they were trained not to feel their own emotions. Written on the article was a note from James' grandmother to his mother which said, "This is what happened to James!"

This timely, inter-generational message passed from his grandmother to his mother and now to James. It encouraged him to continue his inner work to heal the part of himself that had learned to shut down his feelings. He had received validation that he had not been exaggerating his childhood experiences. James' weariness with his personal work evaporated because he had experienced divine intention in the universe and tailored guidance on his growth path.

PRINCIPLE #7:

There is multiplicity of guiding intention in the universe—things are happening to everyone else that are meant to guide them along tailored growth paths.

This principle can be dealt with quite briefly because it simply states that the preceding Principle #6 is true for all of us. As a case in point, when James, in the last example, was explaining his experience of being personally guided along a tailored growth path, he added that his sister experienced different, but equally tailored, forms of being guided along her own growth path through the experience of sorting through the accumulated belongings of their deceased parents.

PRINCIPLE #8:

There is synchronicity designed into life— things that happen to you to guide you along a growth path may be synchronized and intersect with things that are happening to someone else to guide them along a growth path.

It is clear from the preceding evidence that all of us are being guided by our Creator on spiritual growth curricula tailored specifically to our individual needs. Principle #8 brings another level of complexity to these change and growth dynamics by adding that your curriculum and mine may be intertwined—they may be unfolding in synchronized and intersecting ways. In the Watchman

Parable, the lover's curriculum (searching for his beloved) and the beloved's curriculum (searching for the ring she had lost) are synchronized to intersect on the far side of the garden wall.

The Example of Linda & Jake—Having Intertwining Growth Path Curricula

The principle of intertwining curricula is illustrated by the experiences of a sister and brother who became yoked together in a second generation family business that designed, manufactured, and marketed leather handbags and related accessories. Linda, the sister, had worked with her mother, the founder of the business, for eight years and had established herself as the creative force and Director of New Product Development. The mother, who had overseen all aspects of the business for thirty years, suddenly fell ill and had to retire from the business. At about the same time, Jake, the brother, lost his job as a financial analyst due to downsizing in the 2008 recession. The mother promptly hired Jake as Director of Finance, drew up papers making Linda and Jake equal co-owners of the business, and named them co-occupiers of the office of president in addition to their director-level duties.

Jake had been the "golden boy" in the family for whom college grades, money, and continuous advancement in jobs had always come easily. He was critical of others, including family members, had an aloof manner, and was accustomed to controlling things. He was not happy about the prospect of sharing the company leadership equally with his sister. Linda dreaded working with him because she anticipated that he would disrespect her role and experience while trying to take control. One can see that this situation could either turn out to be a disaster for Linda, Jake, and the business or growth-producing for all three. Fortunately, it turned out to be the latter because both Linda and Jake chose to use Wall-Seeking principles to address their issues. They made conscious choices to set their egos and defenses aside and work collaboratively to address each issue as it arose.

Jake gradually learned to honor other people's boundaries and share control with Linda and others. He gained respect and appreciation for Linda's creative talents and business acumen, which were different from his own. He also learned to become more accepting and less critical of other family members and business associates. He became a more humble, collaborative, and compassionate person. All of these gains in awareness and spiritual attributes represented walls Jake had to scale and go over, some on his own and some during collaborative consultation with Linda.

Linda grew as well, also gaining new perspectives, understanding, and spiritual attributes. She learned that her "totally self-assured" brother had self-doubts and weaknesses just like she did, that his aloofness arose out of not knowing how to relate to others in a cooperative, equal manner, and that he felt alone atop the pedestal on which the family and others had placed him. She learned how to replace her self-doubts and resentment for Jake with compassion and to draw him toward growth and self-awareness. She also learned how to assert her views and challenge her brother's thinking when necessary even as she gained increased respect for his skills and talents which were different from, but dovetailed with, her own. All of these gains in awareness and spiritual attributes represented walls Linda had to scale and go over, some on her own and some during collaborative consultation with Jake.

Because both Linda and Jake had used a Wall-Seeking approach to address their forced business relationship, the fact that their individually tailored spiritual growth curricula were intertwined and unfolded in synchronized, intersecting ways *became an asset* rather than a liability. They were able to leverage their intertwining curricula to *accelerate* their individual and collective growth while gaining appreciation for their differences. As an added bonus, their business grew and became more unified.

It is important to realize that whenever two people use collaborative consultation to address a joint issue, two or more of their Wall-Seeking patterns are intersecting either consciously or unconsciously in a synchronized way. This explains why attempting to collaboratively resolve an issue can sometimes be so challenging.

Our next book provides resources and tools to make such tasks easier and more productive.

PRINCIPLE #9:

There is multiple intentioned synchronicity designed into life—synchronized growth path occurrences are happening to all people, and our lives are intersecting in highly complex, multi-dimensional patterns in which we are the "lover" for some, the "beloved" for others, and "watchmen" for still others. In turn, others we encounter potentially play all these roles for us.

Principle #9 adds even more complexity to the change and spiritual growth dynamics of the growth lab of life. Not only are each of us being guided by our Creator on our own tailored spiritual growth curriculum in which your curriculum and mine may be intertwining, but *synchronized* growth path occurrences are happening to all people; and our lives are intersecting in highly complex, multi-dimensional patterns. This means that we all may be experiencing multiple intersecting patterns at any given moment in our lives and that we may be playing different roles in all these intersections—the lover in some, the beloved in others, and the watchman in still others. It also means that other people in these intersecting patterns may be playing all these different roles for us.

At our best, we may be conscious of, and distracted by, two or three intersecting patterns in our lives, but totally unaware of three or four others. No mere human being can completely comprehend the complexity of the full-scale lover/watchmen/beloved dynamics going on in the world. However, God is so powerful and loving that He simultaneously and without omission tends to the tailored spiritual growth needs of each of us. The Watchman Parable suggests this is so, and other Holy Writings confirm it. The Muslim Writings say of God:

> Nothing whatsoever keepeth Him from being occupied with any other thing."[40]

And the Bahá'í Writings state:

> ...His handiwork knoweth neither beginning nor end. The domain of His decree is too vast for the tongue of mortals to describe, or for the bird of the human mind to traverse; and the dispensations of His providence are too mysterious for the mind of man to comprehend.[41]

Despite this mysterious, overwhelming complexity and our human limitations, our job is to manage the intersecting patterns we are aware of in our lives by playing our roles as lover, watchman, or beloved using the Wall-Seeking perspective: striving to achieve the three ultimate purposes of life; leveraging the five directional forces of the spiritual growth lab of life; and using collaborative consultation both within ourselves and with others to resolve issues and foster growth. When we manage our known intersecting patterns in this spiritually optimal way, we tend to address our unknown intersecting patterns constructively as well; and in so doing we draw nearer to our Creator, contribute to our own and other's spiritual growth, and advance civilization. If we imagine a world in which the majority of people were navigating life in this way, we get an inkling of what it would be like to live in a spiritually-centered world civilization.

A Family Example of Wall-Seeker Principle #9 in Action

So that we can better visualize and manage these change and growth dynamics, let us look at a family situation that generally illustrates Wall-Seeking Principle #9. We will not attempt to capture every detail of the family situation or identify lover, watchman, and beloved roles, but simply get a glimpse of how complex the Wall-Seeking dynamics can be in something as small as a family unit.

Jill and Burt are a married couple in their early sixties who have two married children. Their daughter, Ellen, and her husband, Russ, experience the birth of their first baby—the first grandchild of Jill and Burt. Because the young parents both need to work, Jill and Burt volunteer to provide most of the daycare for the new baby, realizing how important the early development years are to a child's physical, spiritual, and psychological well-being. Although Burt is still working full-time in his own business and Jill is working part-time, they adjust their schedules and work out a plan to provide the care for their grandchild during the times when the parents are working.

The program unfolds as planned for several months until Jill experiences the recurrence of a chronic illness which requires that she take an indefinite leave of absence from her profession, eliminate some of her social service activities, and reduce the amount of childcare she is providing. Burt steps up to fill in the needed childcare. The following Wall-Seeking dynamics are generated by these circumstances:

- Jill struggles with the rigors of daycare activities, the loss of her professional identity and the service, self-esteem, and adult collegiality involved, the cessation of her social service activity, and how to deal with her perplexing, often disabling illness.

- Burt struggles with anxieties over Jill's health, the rigors of daycare activities, the constriction of the time available for his work and other activities, a sense of loss of control over his life, and concerns over his ability to generate enough income to assure Jill's and his retirement security.

- Ellen notices the stresses her parents are going through, and it leads to collaborative consultation in the family. As a result, the following changes, activities, and outcomes occur:

  o Russ changes his work schedule so that he can be with his child all day Fridays enabling Jill and Burt to be free of childcare activities on that day.

- o Ellen and her father spend more time together as she comes by after work four days a week to pick up the baby; they talk through family-of-origin and father-daughter issues and achieve an even closer relationship.

- o As is common with new parents, Ellen and Russ reflect on their own and each other's childhoods. They confer about the parenting they received that they want to emulate and things they want to change in order to be even better parents. They share their anxieties and help each other work through unresolved issues from the past.

- In the weeks and months that follow these changes, Russ discovers many new creative and resourceful dimensions in himself as a parent and experiences intense joy in his deepening relationship with his child. Ellen has the joy of seeing her husband blossom as a parent and experiences corresponding enrichment in their marriage relationship.

- Burt discovers that he can adequately sustain his and Jill's income by more tightly scheduling his business activities. He experiences great joy in becoming a close observer and facilitator of the development of his grandchild—experiencing a degree of full involvement that he had long regretted not having with his own children during their early years due to his preoccupation with being the primary wage earner. Like his son-in-law, Burt sees a flowering of his own capacity for providing compassion and nurturing; and this enriches his relationship with Jill and his own children as well. Overall, Burt experiences a degree of life balance that is new and refreshing to him.

- Jill struggles with her health situation. She and Burt have collaborative consultation on this issue and decide:

- o To extend Jill's indefinite leave from her professional work;

- o To investigate new allopathic and holistic approaches to resolving her health issue;

- o To systematically check out referrals to health care resources she has been given by caring friends and acquaintances;

- o To become open to changes in her lifestyle that may be required to accommodate improvements to her health;

- o To reevaluate priorities and time commitments;

- o To execute these explorations together and have them be driven by prayer.

- In the second month following these decisions, Jill and Burt find two new health resources that together affect a dramatic improvement in Jill's health. The circumstances surrounding the discovery of these new resources are highly synchronous—the Wall-Seeking patterns are unmistakable.

- In the process of implementing the advice of these new health resources, Jill makes new discoveries about herself and her inner life that allow her to rebalance her life patterns in profound ways. One manifestation of these changes is that she renews an artistic endeavor that she had put on hold years before and finds it highly refreshing and nurturing to her spirit. Over time, she finds the health and energy to return to the social service activity she had previously been forced to suspend.

It should be apparent from the preceding description (illustrating Wall-Seeking Principle #9) that the intersecting and synchronized Wall-Seeking patterns of multiple people ripple out from an originating event—in this case, the birth of a child—like the effects of a stone tossed into a lake. The waves ripple out one after the other in a repeating pattern that seems without end. Each person has distinct walls to scale, beloveds to seek and roles to play—including watchman, lover and beloved—in relation to each of the others; but all participate in a synchronized, intersecting dance of spiritual aspiration, testing, and growth.

This sample illustration focused on only some of the testing and growth ramifications for some members of a single family, but the effects continued on beyond our description. For example, Jill's extended leave of absence from her work caused her clients to go through the struggle of finding another helping resource; and the childcare rigors Burt and Jill experienced caused Ellen's younger sister to pitch in to help with the childcare, which helped her grow in preparation for her own future parenting role. The ripples of testing and growth opportunities—of lovers, watchmen, walls, and beloveds—that flow from one change in a single life, challenge and affect countless others.

However, this rippling flow of opportunities depends on the willingness of the participants to leverage the opportunities for growth as Wall-Seekers. At any moment, Ellen, Russ, Jill, or Burt could have stonewalled, become defensive or critical of others, and resisted the testing and growth opportunities flowing their way. They could have remained static despite the rippling flow going on around them. Instead, they manifested the combination of *intending to grow* and *going with the flow* that is required of Wall-Seekers. They trusted in God, committed to the three purposes of life, looked honestly at their thoughts and feelings, shared them with each other, and used collaborative consultation to deal with issues in their intersecting Wall-Seeking patterns in a spiritually optimal way.

It is important to realize that when an entire family—or any group of people—come together to use collaborative consultation to address an issue, one or more Wall-Seeking patterns of each individual may begin consciously or unconsciously intersecting and synchronizing with the Wall-Seeking patterns of all the other people. To provide adequate group infrastructure to constructively leverage the complexities of all these opportunities for growth, the group members will be helped by applying the principles and processes described in our next book.

PRINCIPLE #10:

We should welcome the watchmen in our lives—it is a waste of time and energy to try to determine if they are motivated by love or wrath.

We have noted that the watchmen in the parable, who seemed to the lover to be driving him *off course* in terms of his goal, were actually driving him *on course* in terms of his spiritual journey. Wall-Seeking Principle #10 states that it makes no difference whether the watchmen are motivated by love, wrath, or any other emotion; their impacts are still valuable to us if we welcome them, or at least accept them with peaceful resignation, into our lives. In many cases, the watchmen in our lives may be "simply doing their jobs," but their impact on us has the potential to spark our spiritual growth—so long as we welcome their influence. The following poem by Rumi captures this spirit:

The Guesthouse

By Rumi

This being human is a guesthouse.
Every morning a new arrival.

A joy, a depression, a meanness,
some momentary awareness comes
as an unexpected visitor.

Welcome and entertain them all!
Even if they're a crowd of sorrows,
who violently sweep your house
empty of its furniture,

still, treat each guest honorably.
He may be clearing you out
for some new delight.
The dark thought, the shame, the malice,
meet them at the door laughing,
and invite them in.

Be grateful for whoever comes,
because each has been sent
as a guide from beyond. [42]

One of the great challenges of dealing with watchmen in our lives is that they tend to bring us things that—on their face—we do not want. Once the lover in the Watchman Parable headed for the marketplace in search of relief and his beloved, the last thing he wanted was obstruction. In our lives, the watchmen may show up as getting laid off or fired from a job, losing an opportunity that we had longed for, having a friend or loved one cast us aside, getting sick, being trapped in a situation we can't seem to get out of, missing a key meeting or an event we urgently desired to attend, or being made to look ridiculous in an embarrassing social situation, etc. Watchmen—whether they are people, events, or conditions—have a knack for running counter to our will. Our culturally conditioned response will be to become consumed with the social/political ramifications of the situation—to find who to blame, get angry toward ourselves or others, or plan how to get even and fight the good fight. However, Wall-Seekers remain mindful of the previously referenced scriptural admonition to:

> Ask not of Me that which We desire not for thee,
> then be content with what We have ordained for
> thy sake, for this is that which profiteth thee, if
> therewith thou dost content thyself. [43]

It is not that the Wall-Seeker ignores the circumstances presented by the watchmen or takes no responsibility in connection with them, but that she or he begins with **contentment**—an acceptance that these circumstances represent a personally tailored curriculum from the Creator for spiritual growth in the current moment. In adversity, Wall-Seekers ask themselves questions such as:

- What are these circumstances calling upon me to develop in terms of spiritual attributes?

- Rather than my will, what does it seem like God's will is for me at this time?

- What is my heart telling me in response to these circumstances that contradicts what my head and/or emotions may be telling me?

- Considering the three purposes of life and the five directional forces of the spiritual growth lab of life, what reactions would best contribute to spiritual development?

Wall-Seekers learn to look upon the countering of their will by the watchman as *a gift,* and at the detour required in response to the watchman as *a course correction.* Other Holy Writings also confirm us in thinking of watchmen as divine emissaries. The Christian Writings counsel us regarding emissaries who may show up as strangers.

> **Be not forgetful to entertain strangers: for thereby some have entertained angels unawares.** [44]

When we are preoccupied with worldly conditions and neglectful of spiritual reality we can misjudge both situations and emissaries. The Bahá'i Writings describe people in this condition as follows:

> **They have conceived the straight to be crooked, and have imagined their friend an enemy.** [45]

Wall-Seekers choose enlightenment in the context of watchman forces by posing questions to themselves such as:

- In response to these watchman-generated circumstances, how am I mistaking my friend for an enemy?

- In responding to these watchman-generated forces, is there a pathway I perceive to be crooked that actually is the straight path?

- Given these watchman-generated circumstances, is there a stranger present who could be an angel?

A Case in Point

In 1968, during the Vietnam War, Bill was inducted into the US Army. Having been an English major and anticipating an absence of intellectual stimulation during basic and advanced training, Bill packed a dozen classic paperback books to read during his spare moments in the months ahead. At the induction center at Fort Polk, Louisiana, the drill sergeants had all of the inductees disembark from the buses in the parking lot and dump out the contents of their duffle bags on the pavement. They removed drugs, weapons, and other contraband wherever they found it—and, for some reason, they removed all of the books Bill had brought from home. He was left with only one book, a Bible that had been handed to him by the Gideons (an organization that distributes Bibles to hotels and people in distressing circumstances) when he arrived at the airport at Fort Polk earlier in the day.

Bill knew nothing about Wall-Seeking at the time and felt outraged by the "watchmen" who had removed his books. However, realizing that complaining to a drill sergeant on the first day of active duty was not likely to have a good outcome, he had no recourse; he had to accept what occurred. Trying to calm down, and looking down at the isolated Gideon's Bible on the pavement, he thought, *maybe the next several months are an opportunity to read the Bible from cover to cover and get my spiritual life in order.* That is exactly what he did during that time, and the seeking and scriptural study pattern he established led him to the discovery of the essential oneness of all the world's revealed religions by the end of his active duty period in the army. It proved to be the most valuable *gift* and *course correction* of his lifetime. This was an early Wall-Seeker experience for a person who, up to that time, had not normally dealt very wisely with watchmen.

The Wall-Seeking skills of welcoming watchmen in our lives and ignoring whether they are motivated by love or wrath also show up during collaborative consultation when we confer on issues. The watchmen may show up as someone's idea that runs counter to our own thinking, or as a person who demonstrates some dimension of diversity that we have not yet learned how to accept. Here too, we need to be vigilant that we are not mistaking a friend for an enemy.

PRINCIPLE #11:

The goal in life is to grow spiritually—to use the watchmen in our lives to quickly identify the walls we need to scale for change and spiritual growth, and then to go over them as rapidly as possible.

Despite the fact that watchmen and wall patterns are continually coming our way in life, we are also given freedom of choice over how we respond to these patterns. Some people choose to use the spiritual growth lab of life as an amusement park to feed their lower nature, meanwhile starving their true self or higher nature. Entire lives can be squandered in this way with little or no spiritual growth emerging.

Most people, however, use their freedom of choice to *gradually* grow spiritually from their life experiences. We might describe this process as "learning the hard way" and it is well described in this poem by Portia Nelson.

Autobiography in Five Short Chapters

I.
I walk down the street.
There is a deep hole in the sidewalk.
I fall in
I am lost... I am helpless
It isn't my fault.
It takes forever to find a way out.

II.
I walk down the same street.
There is a deep hole in the sidewalk.
I pretend I don't see it.
I fall in again.
I can't believe I am in the same place.
but it isn't my fault.
It still takes a long time to get out.

III.
I walk down the same street.
There is a deep hole in the sidewalk.
I see it is there.
I still fall in... it's a habit.
my eyes are open
I know where I am.
It is my fault.
I get out immediately.

IV.
I walk down the same street.
There is a deep hole in the sidewalk.
I walk around it.

V.
I walk down another street. [46]

This profound poem describes a praiseworthy pattern—the gradual awakening to our responsibility for our own spiritual growth. However, the object of Wall-Seeking is to *accelerate* this process—to learn the fast way. The Wall-Seeker seeks to move from Chapter I of the poem directly to Chapter V. Armed with the resources described in this book, he or she learns to rapidly identify watchmen and wall patterns in order to scale walls at an optimum rate. Wall-Seekers may be likened to swimmers in the ocean of life who quickly learn to stop fighting the waves, then to swim with the waves, then to bodysurf the waves, and finally to surfboard the waves. They learn to recognize, leverage, and navigate the spiritual growth currents designed into life to propel their acquisition of spiritual attributes and ability to serve others in ways that advance civilization. Their ultimate objective and motivating force is nearness to the Creator.

Granted, there may be some walls in life that Wall-Seekers can scale in a day while others may require years; but time is not lost dancing away from wall recognition. Quickly identifying the walls we need to go over for change and spiritual growth requires that we cultivate relentless honesty with ourselves. The tendencies to protect our comfortable inclinations and blame or argue with watchmen must be replaced with the habit of asking, *what gap in my spiritual growth am I being called to fill by these circumstances?* The Christian Writings call us to this kind of honesty with ourselves.

> For I say, through the grace given unto me, to every man that is among you, not to think of himself more highly than he ought to think; but to think soberly, according as God hath dealt to every man the measure of faith. [47]

And the Bahá'í Writings do likewise.

> It is my hope that you may consider this matter, that you may search out your own imperfections and not think of the imperfections of anybody else.

Strive with all your power to be free from imperfections. Heedless souls are always seeking faults in others. What can the hypocrite know of others' faults when he is blind to his own? ... As long as a man does not find his own faults, he can never become perfect. Nothing is more fruitful for man than the knowledge of his own shortcomings. The Blessed Perfection says, "I wonder at the man who does not find his own imperfections."[48]

PRINCIPLE #12:

The difficulties and suffering we experience in life are intended to lead us away from self-absorption & limitation, and toward reliance on divine assistance and the infinite.

While knowing, loving, and relying on God is one of the three purposes of life, simply living in the world does not enable us to achieve it. On our own, we humans become self-absorbed and have only limited access to our potential.

Learning to Rely on Divine Assistance

It is only through the guidance of the Messengers of God that have been sent to humanity through the ages that we learn to know our Creator, rely on His assistance, and gain access to our full potential as spiritual beings. The Muslim Writings describe the human condition that the divine Messengers come to address through Their guidance and assistance.

God desires to lighten things for you, for man was created a weakling. [49]

And the Bahá'i Writings describe the condition of humanity when this guidance and assistance is not accessed.

...the people are wandering in the paths of delusion, bereft of discernment to see God with their own eyes, or hear His Melody with their own ears. [50]

Recognition of our need for divine assistance and guidance is a hard lesson to learn for many; and even those who have learned it are susceptible to forgetting it. The allurements of the world are a test that can distract us from knowledge of, and reliance on, our Creator. When we become engaged with the world without reference to our purpose of knowing and loving God, we become reliant on self, attached to the contingent world, unmindful of our spiritual nature, and wanderers in the "paths of delusion." In this state, we are drawing our sustenance from worldly rather than divine sources and feeding our lower rather than higher nature. We may become highly skilled at scaling *worldly and material heights* while completely avoiding the scaling of *spiritual walls*. A life spent in such delusion is the opposite of Wall-Seeking; and, using gold as a metaphor for worldly attachment, the Bahá'í Writings say:

O Son of Man! Thou dost wish for gold and I desire thy freedom from it. Thou thinkest thyself rich in its possession, and I recognize thy wealth in thy sanctity therefrom. By My life! This is My knowledge, and that is thy fancy; how can My way accord with thine? [51]

The Writings of Islam state what the source of our sustenance should be.

God is the best to take care of man, and He is the Most Merciful of those who show mercy! [52]

The Hindu Writings also make the case for accessing divine, rather than worldly sustenance.

God the Rescuer,
God the Savior,

Almighty, whom we joyfully adore,
Powerful God,
Invoked by all men,
May he, the bounteous, grant us his blessings! [53]

And the Zoroastrian Writings emphasize the transformative power of divine assistance.

Through Thy power, O Lord,
Make life renovated, real at Thy will.[54]

The Role of Difficulties & Suffering

Many of the difficulties and suffering we experience in life are meant to detach us from self-centeredness and worldly attachment, and bring us to the realization that we are fragile creatures who need to rely on divine assistance in order to unlock our spiritual potential. The Judaic Writings convey this truth.

Come, let us return to the Lord;
for he has torn, that he may heal us;
he has stricken, and he will bind us up.
After two days he will revive us;
on the third day he will rise us up,
that we may live before him. [55]

The Hindu Writings also emphasize the saving grace of divine assistance.

We who live in the world, still attached to karmas,
can overcome the world by thy grace alone.[56]

The Christian Writings emphasize the unwavering reliability of God's assistance to us despite our weaknesses.

If we are faithless, he remains faithful—for he cannot deny himself. [57]

In a revealed prayer in the Bahá'í Writings, we find these words:

> I know of a certainty, by virtue of my love for Thee, that Thou wilt never cause tribulations to befall any soul unless Thou desirest to exalt his station in Thy earthly life with the bulwark of Thine all-compelling power, that it may not become inclined toward the vanities of this world. [58]

The Outcome of Detachment from the Contingent World

Like the lover in the Watchman Parable who evolves through tribulation from self-reliant preoccupation with the contingent world to reliance on his Creator and the world of the spirit, our own difficulties and suffering in the growth lab of life reveal to us our own powerlessness and God's might, our own poverty and God's wealth. Suffering opens us to awareness of our spiritual nature and its reliance on divine assistance for sustenance. As we travel this awareness path, we begin to understand spiritual truths that contradict our learning from the contingent world. For example, we stop defining success in the context of acquiring worldly comforts and pleasures and start appreciating the spiritual value of detachment from these things. We realize that the process of identifying, scaling, and throwing ourselves over walls into new awareness is fueled by reliance on the divine and inhibited by reliance on the worldly.

In addition to the parable, other Holy Writings emphasize the value of detaching from the contingent world. The Hindu Writings say:

> A complete disregard for all worldly things, perfect contentment, abandonment of hope of every kind, and patience—these constitute the highest food of one who has subjugated his senses and acquired a knowledge of Self. No need of attaching yourself to things of this world. Attachment to worldly objects is productive of evil. [59]

The Buddhist Writings state:

> Come, behold this world which is like unto an or-
> namented royal chariot, wherein fools flounder,
> but for the wise there is no attachment. [60]

The Christian Writings say:

> Do not be conformed to this world, but be trans-
> formed by the renewal of your mind, that you may
> prove what is the will of God, what is good and ac-
> ceptable and perfect. [61]

The Muslim Writings advise:

> Be in the world as if you were a stranger or a trav-
> eler. [62]

And the Bahá'í Writings warn:

> Whatsoever deterreth you, in this Day, from loving
> God is nothing but the world. Flee it, that ye may
> be numbered with the blest. [63]

These same Writings give us a word picture describing a person's unlimited condition of detachment from the world and reliance on divine assistance and the infinite.

> Blessed is the man who hath detached himself
> from all else but Me, hath soared in the atmo-
> sphere of My love, hath gained admittance into My
> Kingdom, gazed upon My realms of glory, quaffed
> the living waters of My bounty, hath drunk his fill
> from the heavenly river of My loving providence,
> acquainted himself with My Cause, apprehended
> that which I concealed within the treasury of My
> Words, and hath shone forth from the horizon of di-
> vine knowledge engaged in My praise and glorifi-
> cation. Verily, he is of Me. Upon him rest My mercy,

My loving-kindness, My bounty and My glory.[64]

The distance to be traveled in moving from self-centered "wandering in the paths of delusion" to detached soaring "in the atmosphere of My love" is a formidable one, most often traveled gradually. And this journey of increasing detachment is not achieved by retreating from the world, but by operating in it to achieve the three ultimate purposes of life in our own unique way.

The Crucible of God's Love

On this pathway, some of us go through periods of such intense suffering and difficulties in life that it seems beyond all proportion to the goals of spiritual growth and closeness to the Creator. However, wise wayfarers realize that in these trials we are experiencing the *crucible* of God's love—that we are being purified and recreated by this testing process.

The word "crucible" comes from a Latin word meaning an earthen pot for melting metals. The crucible of God's love uses earthly circumstances to melt and purify our lower nature so that our spiritual nature can shine through. The Bahá'í Writings (this time using gold as a metaphor for spiritual attributes) say:

> Not until man is tried doth the pure gold distinctly separate from the dross. Torment is the fire of test wherein the pure gold shineth resplendently and the impurity is burned and blackened.[65]

This quotation, with its metal refining metaphor, seems to echo a similar quotation from the Judaic Writings describing God's method of growing us spiritually and teaching us to rely on divine assistance.

> And He shall sit as a refiner and purifier of silver.[66]

When silver is refined, the refiner must hold the piece of silver in the middle of the fire where flames are the hottest in order to burn the impurities away. The refiner must hold and watch the silver continuously because if it is held in the flame a moment too long, it can be destroyed. The refiner knows the silver is completely refined when he can see his image in it. So it is with our spiritual growth processes. God holds us in the fire—never testing us beyond what He knows our capacity to be—until self-reliance and finite qualities give way to divine reliance and spiritual qualities that reflect God's image.

Other Holy Writings support the fact that God does not test us beyond our limits. The Christian Writings state:

> God is faithful, and he will not let you be tempted beyond your strength, but with the temptation will also provide the way of escape, that you may be able to endure it.[67]

The Muslim Writings assure us that:

> God asks nothing of any soul save that which He has given it.[68]

The Mystery of Suffering, the Power of Patience

Despite these scriptural assurances, some of us experiencing difficulties will feel like we are being tested beyond our limits and are completely alone. At such times, we find ourselves grappling with the mystery of suffering in this world. Author and historian Adib Taherzadeh shares relevant insights.

> In his life, man experiences many trials and tribulations, but often does not understand their purpose. Although the full significance of suffering cannot be fully appreciated in this world, its effects upon the individual can be readily observed.
>
> In the world of nature most objects are affected by external influences. For instance, a piece of iron left on its own is cold and becomes rusty. As a result of friction, however, it produces heat, its surface

becomes shiny, and by increasing the force of friction, it can become a luminous body. But only pressure from without will cause these characteristics, which are latent within the iron, to be manifested.

Similarly, within a human being there are many qualities and virtues which remain dormant. Often, suffering helps to release the potentialities within man, bringing to the surface noble qualities which had hitherto remained concealed. History has shown that many eminent men have achieved greatness merely by facing hardships and difficulties. Through perseverance and steadfastness, they have overcome obstacles, demonstrated their strength of character and revealed the hidden powers latent within them... The greater the cause, the more strenuous are the tests and trials to which the individual is subjected. [69]

The Holy Writings emphasize that those who persevere patiently and with long suffering through tribulation will receive a great reward. As previously referenced, the Bahá'í Writings state:

> **Blessed are the steadfastly enduring, they that are patient under ills and hardships, who lament not over anything that befalleth them, and who tread the path of resignation....[70]**

And in the Writings of Islam, the recompense for patient perseverance is said to be limitless.

> **Those who patiently persevere will truly receive a reward without measure. [71]**

In the end, Wall-Seekers experiencing suffering learn to have faith that God knows our limits better than we do, and that they are being held close in the loving hand of God and watched intensely by the compassionate eye of the Creator as their spiritual refinement process is underway. They recognize that being in the crucible of God's love is the *safest* place to be. As the Bahá'í Writings say:

> O Son of Being! My love is My stronghold; he that entereth therein is safe and secure, and he that turneth away shall surely stray and perish.[72]

PRINCIPLE #13:
Having both self-compassion and compassion for others deepens understanding.

The Holy Writings of all the revealed religions instruct us to manifest compassion and kindness to all human beings. As discussed earlier, compassion is similar to empathy, but it also includes the desire to alleviate the suffering—whether of others or ourselves—through action. The Hindu Writings state:

> What sort of religion can it be without compassion?
> You need to show compassion to all living beings.
> Compassion is the root of all religious faiths.[73]

The Jewish Writings proclaim:

> The world stands upon three things: upon the Law, upon worship, and upon kindness.[74]

The Buddhist Writings say:

> The bodhisattva should adopt the same attitude toward all beings, his mind should be even toward all beings, he should not handle others with an uneven mind, but with a mind which is friendly, well-disposed, helpful, free from aversions, avoid-

ing harm and hurt; he should handle others as if they were his mother, father, son, or daughter.[75]

The Christian Writings advise:

> Do not rebuke an older man but exhort him as you would a father; treat younger men like brothers, older women like mothers, younger women like sisters, in all purity.[76]

The Muslim Writings state:

> All [human] creatures are God's children, and those dearest to God are those who treat His children kindly.[77]

The modern era is filled with conflict—conflict in which each side exaggerates the positives of its own side and the negatives of the other side. Differences are played up to such an extreme that there can be no understanding because compassion and kindness are absent. Speaking to the condition of humanity in the modern era, the Bahá'í Writings say:

> No two men can be found who may be said to be outwardly and inwardly united. The evidences of discord and malice are apparent everywhere, though all were made for harmony and union. The Great Being saith: O well-beloved ones! The tabernacle of unity hath been raised; regard ye not one another as strangers. Ye are the fruits of one tree, and the leaves of one branch.[78]

The essence of compassion is seeing with this eye of oneness, which creates a different paradigm of seeking those things upon which we agree rather than disagree. To counter "discord and malice" seems to require that we use compassion to become *outwardly* united with others by way of actions, *inwardly* united with each other by way of the heart, and *inwardly* united with ourselves by way of the subordination of our lower nature to the leadership of our true selves. Compassion leads us to a higher level of understanding, one aspect of which is the recognition that we "...all were made for harmony and union."

The Messengers of God teach us that surrounding all of the apparent *hardness* of existence is the *softness* of compassion. They charge us with the task of bringing the softness of compassion to the human interface in the contingent world so that it mirrors the conditions in the spiritual world. This is an important element of fulfilling the life purpose of carrying forward an ever-advancing civilization because it involves infusing the material with that which is spiritual. The Holy Writings emphasize the role of compassionate behavior in enhancing the life of society. The Hindu Writings say:

> The same thing does the divine voice here, thunder, repeat, Da! Da! Da! that is, restrain yourselves, give, be compassionate. One should practice this same triad, self-restraint, giving, compassion. [79]

The Judaic Writings state:

> A man should share in the distress of the community, for so we find that Moses, our teacher, shared in the distress of the community. [80]

The Christian Writings declare:

> Bear one another's burdens, and so fulfill the law of Christ. [81]

And the Muslim Writings proclaim:

> The best of men are those who are useful to others. [82]

Bringing Forth the Softness of Compassion in the Parable & in Wall-Seeking

In the Watchman Parable, we see the process of bringing the softness of compassion to the human interface begin to unfold even *be-*

fore the lover has become a Wall-Seeker. Self-compassion arises in his heart—his heart laments—only *after* his heart has been "worn to a sigh" and he has wrestled intensely with the watchmen as adversaries. Once his softening experience of self-compassion occurs, it seems to fuel his identification and scaling of the garden wall. This, in turn, leads to his discovery of the beloved, which fills him with compassion for God and everyone else. As a result of this softening, he achieves dramatically higher levels of understanding.

Unlike the lover's initial approach in the Watchman Parable, Wall-Seekers attempt to cultivate compassion inwardly and outwardly *from the start*. Instead of waiting until their hearts are "worn to a sigh" and wrestling with the watchmen as adversaries, they recognize the Wall-Seeking dynamics unfolding and soften with compassion for themselves and the watchmen *early on*. They do this because they have a passion for achieving higher levels of understanding and they know that compassion frames the pathway.

Two Examples from Life—Bringing Compassion to the Human Interface

One of our clients worked in a family business. He suffered distress, anger, and sadness working with his father who habitually made insensitive, harsh comments to him. Recognizing Wall-Seeking dynamics in this situation, we encouraged him to *proactively* cultivate compassion for himself and his father as a starting point. Part of this effort involved having enough self-compassion to reach out to confer with his mother about his distress. In addition, he wanted to understand his father better, so he asked his mother what she knew about his father's childhood.

Among the things she recalled was that his father's mother had told her that, after his father's parents divorced, the divorced father seldom visited the family. On several occasions, beginning when the boy was five years old, however, the father was scheduled to pick up his son for an afternoon together. Each time, the boy would wait excitely at the edge of the street for the father's arrival, but the father never came. The boy was crestfallen each time this happened.

Hearing this story about his father's childhood filled our client with compassion for his father. This, in turn, enabled him to better understand what was beneath his father's insensitive behavior—that he had hardened his heart in order to withstand his childhood pain. This increased compassion and understanding allowed our client to take his father's comments less personally and led to less distressing, more effective communication between the two, which also improved the climate within the business.

A second example illustrating the virtuous cycle of self-compassion, leading to both compassion for others and higher understanding, involved one of our clients who was in a support group. After one of the sessions, he sent us the following message:

> I thought I would share with you something I noticed after the last group meeting. During the meeting, X was talking about how influential his older brother had been in his growing up—always patiently showing him how to do things on almost a project-like basis. The story made me feel compassion for X and his brother.

> This led me to feel compassion for myself when I realized that the reason I frequently find myself irritated with people when I have to show them how to do things is because I didn't have anyone who showed me things when I was growing up. I always had to figure things out myself. Therefore, I have no model for being a teacher/mentor, and I assume that everyone should be able to puzzle through problems without assistance.

> Anyway, I've been really, really, really annoyed with someone I work with because I always have to show her how to do everything. On the one hand, I don't expect everyone to know how to do everything. On

the other hand, I expect an internal consultant (as she is) to be superior in skill and ability and to be a "self-starter" who requires minimum hand-holding. Anyway, I was really dreading interaction with her because it always made me so angry. But after that meeting, I find that it's almost like a switch flipped in my personality, and I no longer want to reach for the claw-hammer every time she walks over. It must be heightened awareness or something.

Our client was able to develop compassion for himself by reflecting on the sadness and pain he experienced from having no one to spend the time to teach and help him figure things out as he was growing up. Once he recognized this unresolved issue from his past and had compassion for himself, he experienced compassion for others and no longer felt angry with people he was called upon to teach and help. They had served as watchmen by making him so frustrated that he sought out a support group. And in that group, he had heard a story that evoked compassion and deeper understanding of his own feelings. He had gone over a wall which released him from experiencing these negative feelings. On the other side of that wall he found a beloved in the form of freedom to serve, higher understanding, and a sense of calm and peace. A few years later he discovered a secondary beloved issuing from his continuing Wall-Seeking in the form of a successful business he founded, which was dependent on a special skill that had emerged in him—a passion for patiently teaching and mentoring others.

PRINCIPLE #14:

In resolving issues, collaborative consultation informed by divine assistance results in greater understanding and spiritual growth than does adversarial contention.

Wall-Seekers see collaborative consultation as the preferred process to be used by individuals and groups for solving problems, sharing perspectives, considering possibilities, generating greater understanding, and making decisions that are conducive to spiritual growth. They also recognize that consultation fosters unity of purpose among highly diverse participants. To be effective, however, this procedure needs to begin with prayers for divine assistance and requires an atmosphere of compassion among participants. As the lover in the Watchman Parable discovered on the other side of the wall, it is the *combination* of divine assistance, compassion, and the collaborative interpenetration of ideas that enables the recasting of problems and dilemmas into opportunities for spiritual growth and social advancement. Consultation converts separation, confusion, and conflict into unified, wise, and just solutions founded on spiritual principles. As stated earlier, an in-depth exploration of the consultation process is beyond the scope of this book, but the following illustration will show examples of the steps and principles that may be used.

A Family Example—Consultation Deepens Understanding & Fosters Growth

We have often used collaborative consultation in our family to come to decisions both large and small. One of those times occurred when Bill's mother had a serious stroke, and after ten months of physical therapy interspersed with additional strokes, she passed away. It was just before school started in the fall for our daughters Erin and Laura when the four of us decided to try and salvage part of the summer by renting a cottage on a lake in northern Minnesota. All of us were weary and sad about Bill's mother. We felt emotionally raw.

During the vacation, Bill said to the family one morning that he had been sleepless most of the night. He felt like his head and his heart were contending—his head saying he needed to stay on his current path, and his heart saying something was missing and he needed to take stock of his life. Feeling somewhat sheepish about interrupting the vacation with a personal problem, Bill asked if the family would collaboratively consult with him so that he could sort out his confusion. Erin, Laura, and Jean consented immediately. The room was full of compassion because we all were mindful of the distress and suffering the others had been through in the preceding months and wanted to alleviate that distress.

We began with prayers for divine assistance, and then Bill opened up about his feelings and thoughts. He said that seeing his mother's life ebb away in the preceding months had made him mindful of the shortness of life; and he felt there was something missing from his own life. He felt that he was not bearing fruit in a way that he needed to bear fruit, but he wasn't sure what it was. On the other hand, he thought that his life with the family, his faith community, and his work was so full that he couldn't imagine how anything else could be squeezed into his life. After a little more discussion, the family articulated the issue Bill was facing as follows: *How can I bear fruit in my life even more meaningfully without short-changing my family, faith community, and clients?*

The family turned to identifying the facts of Bill's situation, which included scientifically verifiable data, but also his thoughts, feelings, and hunches about the terrain surrounding the issue statement. This discussion turned up a sizeable amount of information, but key parts of the information were: wasted time did still exist in Bill's weekly schedule that could be turned to a new endeavor; and Bill's previously unarticulated feeling that he needed to bear fruit through writing because this had been his goal as a teenager and young adult, but life had seemed to take him in a different direction.

Now the family identified spiritual principles that related to the previously agreed upon issue and facts. Among those identified, were the following:

> Planted in the house of the Lord, they shall flourish in the courts of our God. They shall still bring forth fruit in old age; they shall be full of sap and richness.[83] (Judaism)

> For the fruit of the Spirit is in all goodness and righteousness and truth.[84] (Christianity)

And (We bring forth) gardens of grapes, and the olive and the pomegranate, alike and unlike. Look upon the fruit thereof, when they bear fruit, and upon its ripening. Lo! herein verily are portents for a people who believe.[85] (Islam)

Such arts and sciences, however, as are productive of good results, and bring forth their fruit, and are conducive to the well-being and tranquility of men have been, and will remain, acceptable before God.[86] (Bahá'í Faith)

Next, the family identified and agreed upon solutions to the issue that aligned with the agreed upon facts and spiritual principles. During this deliberation, Erin named two books Bill had read in the previous year that had inspired him and asked, "What writing subject is there for you that is related to the themes in those books?" Laura said, "The work you are doing in organization development and life coaching is part of your subject. What is there at the core of that work that you could write about?" Jean said, "You have been journaling for years. There is a mountain of material there. Why don't you draw from it? What is there in the journals that aligns with the themes Erin and Laura just named?" Together, we forged answers to these questions.

This collaborative consultation in a highly compassionate atmosphere took place in about forty-five minutes, and from it came the plan that led to this book and the second one. In order to create an implementation plan, we consulted for another fifteen minutes and agreed that Bill should:

- Start reserving from 6:30-8:30 p.m. each evening as writing time that no one would interrupt;

- Start thinking of himself as a writer and telling people about his writing—the same way he did when he redefined himself professionally and launched the consulting and coaching business;

- Lean on the encouragement that Jean, Erin, and Laura would provide;

- Rely on Jean as a collaborator and co-author.

As a result of this one-hour collaborative consultation session:

- Bill felt totally at peace in his mind and heart;

- He received an important life course correction;

- He received wisdom and much greater understanding about himself;

- He found a new pathway to increased spiritual growth and service;

- He was delighted to receive Jean as a collaborator and co-author;

- Bill and Jean were struck by how useful and valuable their daughters' contributions to the process had been;

- Their daughters gained insight into the fact that adults also have struggles in life;

- And their daughters experienced further learning about how peaceful and productive family problem solving could be, and received a model to emulate in their future families.

Such is the power of divine assistance combined with compassion and consultation. As previously stated, our next book focuses entirely on this powerful process. In that book, we refer to this process as "Compassionate Consultation."

PRINCIPLE #15:
The key to aligning being and doing in our lives is seeing the end in the beginning.

The Watchman Parable tells us that we should "see the end in the beginning." For Wall-Seekers, this means that each moment of our lives needs to increasingly *begin* with mindfulness about what is the *end* or purpose of life so that we can live a purposeful life. Seeing the end in the beginning starts with awareness of our soul's journeying context; its passage is navigated from the world of the womb, through this material world, to a spiritual world beyond this one. This awareness prevents us from forgetting that we are all spiritual beings having a material experience. The Holy Writings persistently remind us of this truth. The Hindu Writings say:

> The Self cannot be pierced with weapons or burned with fire; water cannot wet it, nor can the wind dry it. The Self cannot be pierced or burned, made wet or dry. It is everlasting and infinite, standing on the motionless foundation of eternity. The Self is unmanifested, beyond all thought, beyond all change. Knowing this, you should not grieve. [87]

The Writings of Judaism state:

> The dust returns to the earth as it was, and the spirit returns to God who gave it. [88]

The Christian Writings say:

> Though our outer nature is wasting away, our inner nature is being renewed every day. For this slight momentary affliction is preparing us for an eternal weight of glory beyond all comparison, because we look not to the things that are seen but to the things that are unseen; for the things that are seen are transient, but the things that are unseen are eternal. [89]

The Writings of Islam proclaim:

> And among His signs is this; you see the earth barren and desolate, but when We send down rain to

it, it is stirred to life and yields increase. Truly, He who gives life to the dead earth can surely give life to men who are dead. For He has power over all things. [90]

And the Bahá'í Writings state:

Verily I say, the human soul is exalted above all egress and regress. It is still, and yet it soareth; it moveth, and yet it is still. It is, in itself, a testimony that beareth witness to the existence of a world that is contingent, as well as to the reality of a world that hath neither beginning nor end. [91]

Navigating this interplay between the contingent world and the spiritual world is the journeying context of which we want to remain mindful. Within this context, our ultimate purposes in life are three: to know and love God; to acquire spiritual attributes; and to carry forward an ever-advancing civilization. In terms of these three purposes, seeing the end in the beginning means that we deliberately design our lives so that our unique gifts, talents, and energies are centered on things that move us forward optimally on these three ultimate purposes. In these ways, our *being* and *doing* become more aligned. Our heart, mind, and spirit—aspects of our *being*—are focused on our soul's journey and the three ultimate purposes of life; and our words, actions, and conduct—the manifestations of our *doing*—spring from, and are aligned with, this focus. The outcome of this greater alignment is joy because we are doing by choice what our Creator has given us the capacity to do—we are achieving our full potential as spiritual beings. In other words, now that we are here, we are doing what we should be doing.

If we review our life circumstances and realize that we feel blocked from focusing on our soul's journeying context and moving forward on the three ultimate purposes of life, we need to make different choices to either *change* our current circumstances or *reframe* them so that we can see greater potential in them for living a purposeful life. To effectively make these choices, we can use collaborative consultation within ourselves or with trusted others to make decisions that generate greater understanding, wisdom, and spiritual growth. Navigating these changes in our lives is also expedited by prayer, reading scripture, meditation, fasting, service to others, and application of the fifteen Wall-Seeking Principles.

The Example of Mario—Making Different Choices to See the End in the Beginning

A client of ours named Mario was married, had a close-knit family, had retired early on a good pension, and was miserable. His wife was still working in a field she felt passionate about. He had worked for a government agency for most of his career, had felt all right about the work, but had looked forward to retiring and being free to do what he wanted to do. He wasn't clear about what he wanted to do in retirement, but assumed he would figure it out easily.

As things turned out, it wasn't so easy. Mario did chores in and around the house, pursued some of his life-long hobbies, watched an increasing amount of television, and tried to exercise and stay in shape. With the passage of time, he experienced less and less motivation. His life-long hobbies didn't satisfy him like they had, his willpower to exercise abandoned him, and he found himself pre-occupied with trivial pastimes. Along with these developments, Mario heard a harsh, critical voice inside himself that had always been there, but now was getting louder and louder. The voice said, "I am miserable, it's my own fault, and I don't have a clue what to do about it."

After passing some time in this limbo-like state, Mario had a series of health problems—none of them life-threatening, but all of them distressing. He had a knee problem, then a rotator cuff problem, and then a hip problem. All of them had ultimate solutions, but the pain and suffering they caused increased his distress to the breaking point. In the end, these health problems, added to his pre-existing misery, were the watchmen that led Mario to begin scaling the wall of creating a more meaningful life in retirement.

Our role with Mario was to acquaint him with many of the principles described in this book. Mario then took those principles and ran with them. First, he began meeting for coffee every other week with a good friend who had a spiritual orientation and experience with reshaping his own life. They had deep conversations together—forms of collaborative consultation—on the nature of spiritual growth, what was involved in changing habits, and ways in which they both wanted to grow.

In terms of the first ultimate purpose of life, knowing and loving God, they decided to say prayers and read scripture together each time they met for coffee and committed to praying more regularly when they weren't together. Mario couldn't tell any difference in his life from doing the prayers and readings in the beginning; but as they continued, he started to feel increasing energy that he could commit to his struggle for growth. He felt like a sailing ship that had become becalmed in the middle of the ocean, that suddenly felt a breath of wind rippling through its sails. His friend attributed Mario's feelings to the fact that he was drawing closer to his Creator and receiving assistance in return.

Regarding the second ultimate purpose of life, acquiring spiritual attributes, Mario and his friend talked about what spiritual attributes they wanted to develop further and each selected two attributes he would focus on for each two-week period between their coffee meetings. At the coffee meetings they shared their progress and setbacks with each other and noted how Wall-Seeking patterns were discernable around each of their struggles to grow. One of the attributes Mario worked on developing was compassion for himself and others. As he thought about his soul's journeying context and developed his capacity for self-compassion, the voice of his harsh, inner critic was quieted, and he experienced still more energy for Wall-Seeking activity.

In terms of the third ultimate purpose of life, carrying forward an ever-advancing civilization, Mario's friend already had several service patterns in his life he felt passionate about. However, Mario drew a blank when he tried to think of ways he could fulfill this purpose. Consulting together, they decided that Mario should experiment with volunteer activities to discover one or more that energized him. Mario's first experiment was applying for and being accepted as a volunteer in a local hospital. As he guided patients from one station to another around the hospital and interacted with them along the way, Mario could definitely sense he was making a difference in their lives; but as time went on, the climate of the hospital reminded him so much of his own health problems that he decided this particular service was not his calling.

Mario consulted collaboratively with his friend again and also with his wife to get additional ideas. The next idea he tried was applying for, and being accepted as, a volunteer in an elementary school classroom each Monday. Most of the time, the teacher asked Mario to work one-on-one with individual students to help them learn their letters and increase their spelling and reading skills. After a few weeks of doing this work, Mario's friend asked him how it was going. When Mario shared his experiences, his friend said, "When you described the connections you were making with these children and how happy they were when you would praise their accomplishments, your voice was full of energy, and your eyes positively sparkled. I think you have gone over a wall and found a beloved." Mario knew his friend was right. While working with these children, he could actually feel the advancement of civilization occurring minute to minute, hour to hour, and day to day. As time passed, Mario increased the number of days each week he was in the classroom with the children.

Mario wanted to find one other service pattern to add to his life that would carry forward an ever-advancing civilization, but struggled to find it. One day, when he was having coffee with his friend, the friend complimented him on how open and welcoming Mario was to everyone he encountered. He said, "Every time I arrive here a little late and order my coffee, I scan the coffee shop to find you, and you are usually engaged in conversation with some stranger—no matter what age, gender, race, or level in society—making friends. Did it ever occur to you that doing this consistently and regularly contributes to an ever-advancing civilization? It contributes to peace, harmony, and the consciousness of the oneness of humanity. It creates a happiness ripple effect—person to person—that can move across oceans and continents!"

As soon as his friend said this, Mario had a memory-pop of a time years earlier when he was taking a city bus downtown, with his two teen-aged sons sitting behind him, to a public Christmas Eve event. At one of the stops, a Native American man got on the bus, walked unsteadily down the aisle, and sat down next to Mario. Mario struck up a conversation with the man, learned about his life and background, that he had lost track of his family, and was alone for the holiday season. After some time, the man indicated his stop was coming up, stood up to leave, and then said to Mario, "Mister, thanks for talking to me tonight. Most people who see me look right through me. Thanks for not doing that."

Mario shared this memory with his friend over coffee, saying that he had thought about it many times over the years, and the experience had motivated him to try to connect with all the people he encountered because it might be a force for good in their lives. Mario and his friend realized that Mario had already found, and was already doing, his second service pattern to carry forward an ever-advancing civilization. All he needed to do was become more intentional and regular in doing it. In the end, Mario scheduled a certain amount of his time each week to do what he called "guerilla connecting and friend-making" to reduce the number of lonely people in the world. He found this work to be highly fulfilling and realized it had been a beloved lurking on "the background screen" of his life for many years just waiting to be recognized.

As Mario persisted in his work of focusing on his soul's journeying context and achieving the three ultimate purposes of life in his own unique ways, he continued to experience increases in his energy levels, became adept at identifying and navigating Wall-Seeking patterns, and gradually discovered that he was becoming joyful. The joy remained even during times of distress with watchmen, of scaling walls, of throwing himself into darkness on the other side of the walls, and of discovering beloveds emerging from the darkness. He came to realize that real joy, lasting joy, comes from spiritual behavior, and that his *being* and *doing* were becoming increasingly aligned.

Conclusion

Our souls are on a journey from the wombs of our mothers, through this material world, to a spiritual world beyond this one. This journey is expedited and the path made straight when we focus on achieving the three ultimate purposes of life in our own unique ways. Along the way, our individual growth and transformation patterns will inevitably intersect with, and impact, the patterns of others in ever-widening circles. If we manage the five directional forces and the Wall-Seeking dynamics of the spiritual growth lab of life, we can optimize our own spiritual growth and that of others around us. The purpose of this book has been to offer some insights, tools, and techniques for navigating this journey more effectively.

When we choose this Wall-Seeking way of life, where does it finally lead us? It leads us as lovers toward the ultimate goal of existence, which is reunion with our ultimate Beloved, the Creator. Following this path, we begin to realize that spiritual joy and happiness are no longer found just *beyond* the wall, but in every step of the Wall-Seeking pathway—interacting with the watchmen, identifying and approaching the wall, scaling the wall, and passing beyond the wall.

We also realize, like the lover in the Watchman Parable, that the journey before us will call for more from each of us than we thought we could give. In describing the achievement of this ultimate goal of existence, the Holy Writings make clear both what will be called for and what will be gained:

> The true seeker hunteth naught but the object of his quest, and the lover hath no desire save union with his beloved. Nor shall the seeker reach his goal unless he sacrifice all things. That is, whatever he hath seen, and heard, and understood, all must

he set at naught, that he may enter the realm of the spirit, which is the City of God. Labor is needed, if we are to seek Him; ardor is needed, if we are to drink of the honey of reunion with Him; and if we taste of this cup, we shall cast away the world. [92]

About the Authors

Bill and Jean Harley are the principals of Harley Consulting & Coaching, a Minneapolis human and organization development firm providing coaching, counseling, consultation, education, and group facilitation services to release human and organizational potential in service to others. Jean is a Psychologist and Bill is an organization development consultant and a Certified Personal & Professional Coach. They have been students of the world's religions for fifty years.

Bill and Jean have been married for forty-seven years and have two adult daughters and sons-in-law plus three grandchildren.

Postscript

To receive periodic, additional insights on the subjects in this book, please sign-up at www.billandjeanharley.com. We encourage our readers to share their own Wall-Seeking and collaborative consultation stories, experiences, and needs with us at Contact@Harley-Coaching.com

Bibliography

'Abdu'l-Bahá. *'Abdu'l-Bahá in London*. Chicago: Baha'i Publishing Society, 1921.

'Abdu'l-Bahá. *Foundations of World Unity*. Wilmette, Illinois: Bahá'í Publishing Trust, 1971.

'Abdu'l-Bahá. *Paris Talks*. London: The Bahá'í Publishing Trust, 1995.

'Abdu'l-Bahá, quoted in *The Divine Art of Living*. Wilmette, Illinois: Bahá'í Publishing Trust, 1974.

'Abdu'l-Bahá. *The Promulgation of Universal Peace*. Wilmette, Illinois: Bahá'í Publishing Trust, 1982.

'Abdu'l-Bahá. *The Secret of Divine Civilization*. Wilmette, Illinois: Baha'i Publishing Trust, 1975.

'Abdu'l-Bahá. *Selections from the Writings of 'Abdu'l-Bahá*. Haifa: Baha'i World Centre, 1978.

Ali, A. Yusuf, trans. *The Meaning of the Glorious Qur'an*. Cairo, Egypt: Dar Al-Kitab Al-Masri, 1938.

Babbitt, Irving, trans. *The Dhammapada.* New York: New Directions, 1965.

Bahá'u'lláh, *Epistle to the Son of the Wolf.* Wilmette, Illinois: Baha'i Publishing Trust, 1969.

Baha'u'llah. *Gleanings from the Writings of Bahá'u'lláh.* Wilmette, Illinois: Baha'i Publishing Trust, 1969.

Bahá'u'lláh. *The Hidden Words.* Wilmette, Illinois: Baha'i Publishing Trust, 1970.

Bahá'u'lláh. *The Kitab-i-Iqan, The Book of Certitude.* Wilmette, Illinois: Baha'i Publishing Trust, 1960.

Baha'u'llah. *Prayers and Meditations by Baha'u'llah.* Wilmette, Illinois: Baha'i Publishing Trust, 1969.

Bahá'u'lláh. *The Proclamation of Bahá'u'lláh.* Haifa: Baha'i World Centre, 1967.

Bahá'u'lláh. *The Seven Valleys and the Four Valleys.* Wilmette, Illinois: Baha'i Publishing Trust, 1952.

Baha'u'llah. *Tablets of Bahá'u'lláh revealed after the Kitab-i-Aqdas.* Wilmette, Illinois: Baha'i Publishing Trust, 1988.

Birnbaum, Philip, ed. *The Encyclopedia of Jewish Concepts.* Rockaway Beach, New York: Hebrew Publishing Co., 1964.

Bly, Robert. *Iron John.* Reading, Massachusetts: Addison-Wesley, 1990.

Bose, Abinash Chandra, ed. *Hymns from the Vedas.* Bombay: Asia Publishing House, 1966.

Bridges, William. *Transitions: Making Sense of Life's Changes.* New York: Addison-Wesley Publishing Company, 1980.

Buhler, Georg, trans. *The Laws of Manu*, Sacred Books of the East, vol. 25. Oxford: Clarendon Press, 1886.

Cleary, Thomas F., trans. *The Flower Ornament Scripture: A Translation of the Avatamsaka Sutra*, 3 vols. Boston: Shambhala, 1984-1987.

Consultation: A Compilation. Extracts from the Writings and Utterances of Bahá'u'lláh, 'Abdu'l-Bahá, Shoghi Effendi, and The Universal House of Justice. Compiled by the Research Department of the Universal House of Justice. Wilmette, Illinois: Bahá'í Publishing Trust, 1980.

Darmesteter, James, trans. *The Zend-Avesta, Part 1: The Vendidad*, Sacred Books of the East, vol. 4. Oxford: Clarendon Press, 1887.

Davids, T. W. Rhys and F. L. Woodward, trans. *Kindred Sayings (Samyutta Nikaya).* London: Pali Text Society, 1950-1956.

Duchesne-Guillemin. *The Hymns of Zarathustra.* London: John Murray, 1963.

Easwaran, Eknath, ed. *The Bhagavad Gita.* Petaluma, California: Nilgiri Press, 1985.

Easwaran, Eknath, trans. *The Upanishads.* Petaluma, California: Nilgiri Press, 1985.

Epstein, I., trans. *The Babylonian Talmud.* New York: Sonsino Press, 1948.

Freke, Timothy. *The Tao Book and Card Pack.* New York: Stewart, Tabori, and Chang, 2002.

Herford, R. Travers, ed. *The Ethics of the Talmud: Sayings of the Fathers.* New York: Schocken Books, 1962.

Hume, R. E., trans. *The Thirteen Principals.* Oxford: Oxford University Press, 1931.

Ibrahim, Ezzeddin and Denys, Johnson-Davies, trans. *An-Nawawi's Forty Hadith.* Damascus: Holy Koran Publishing House, 1977.

Insler, S. *The Gathas of Zarathustra,* Acta Iranica 8, vol. 1. Leiden: E. J. Brill, 1975. Interfaith Explorer at www.BahaiResearch.com.

McConnell, Patty. *A Workbook for Healing.* San Francisco: Harper & Row, 1986.

Muhsin Khan, Muhammad, trans. *The Translation of the Meanings of SahthAl-Bukhari.* Chicago: Kazi Publications, 1976-1979.

Nelson, Portia. *There's A Hole In My Sidewalk: The Romance of Self Discovery.* New York: Atria Books, 2002.

Nikhilananda, Swami, trans. *The Upanishads.* New York: Ramakrishna-Vivekananda Center of New York, 1959.

Panikkar, Raimundo, ed. *Mantramanjari: The Vedic Experience.* Berkeley: University of California Press, 1977.

Popov, Linda Kavelin. *The Family Virtues Guide.* New York: The Penguin Group, 1997.

Prabhavanunda, Swami, ed. *Srimad Bhagavatam: The Wisdom of God.* Hollywood, Calif.: Vedanta Press, 1943.

Prabhavanunda, Swami, ed. *The Spiritual Heritage of India.* Hollywood, Calif.: Vedanta Press, 1963.

*The Qur'an (*J. M. Rodwell, M.A., tr.). New York: Everyman's Library, Dutton, 1971.

Radhakrishnan, S. and C.A. Mone, eds. *A Sourcebook in Indian Philosopy.* Princeton: Princeton University Press, 1957.

Rumi, Jalal ad-Din Muhammad, "Not Always On", 1 April 2004, 29 July 2011 http://www.elise.com/weblog/archives/000312guesthouse-rumi.php.

Saddhatissa, H., trans. *The Sutta-Nipata.* London: Curzon Press, 1985.

Shoghi Effendi. *The Advent of Divine Justice.* Wilmette, Illinois: Bahá'í Publishing Trust, 1969.

Taherzadeh, Adib. *The Revelation of Bahá'u'lláh,* Vol. 1. Oxford: George Ronald, 1984.

The Holy Bible, King James Version. New York: Oxford University Press, 1945.

The Holy Bible, Revised Standard Version. New York: National Council of the Churches of Christ in the USA, 1971.

Thera, Narada Maha, trans. *The Dhammapada.* Colombo, Sri Lanka: Vajirarama, 1972.

Townshend, George. *The Heart of the Gospel.* London: George Ronald, 1960.

Twain, Mark. *Pudd'nhead Wilson.* New York: American Publishing Co., 1894.

World Scripture, A Comparative Anthology of Sacred Texts. St. Paul: Paragon House, 1995.

References and Notes

Chapter 1: The Search for Purpose

1. *Vendidad* 10:10.

2. *Qur'an* 30:22.

3. Proverbs 23:7.

4. *The Chandogya Upanishad.*

5. Matthew 5:48.

6. 1 Corinthians 3.16-17.

7. Bahá'u'lláh, *Gleanings from the Writings of Bahá'u'lláh*, p. 287.

Chapter 2: The Three Ultimate Purposes of Life

1. We refer to the Holy Books of the following religions (with the divine Revelators and approximate founding dates in parentheses): Hinduism (Krishna—2000 B. C.), Judaism (Moses—1330 B.C.), Zoroastrianism (Zoroaster—1000 B.C.), Buddhism (Gautama Buddha—560 B.C.), Christianity (Jesus Christ—1 A.D.), Islam (Muhammad—622 A.D.),

the Bábí Faith (The Báb—1844 A.D.), and the Bahá'í Faith (Bahá'u'lláh—1853 A.D.).

2. Deuteronomy 6:5.

3. Matthew 22:37-38.

4. Bahá'u'lláh, *Prayers and Meditations by Bahá'u'lláh*, p, 313.

5. Linda Kavelin Popov, *The Family Virtues Guide*, p. xvi.

6. 'Abdu'l-Bahá, *Foundations of World Unity*, p. 63.

7. *Talmud*, Hullin 92a.

8. Psalms 127:1.

9. *Bhagavad Gita* 3:10-26.

10. Luke 10:33-34.

11. Luke 10:35.

12. *Hadith of Bukhari.*

13. Bahá'u'lláh, *Gleanings from the Writings of Bahá'u'lláh*, p. 215.

14. Bahá'u'lláh, *Gleanings from the Writings of Bahá'u'lláh*, p. 213.

15. Bahá'u'lláh, *Tablets of Bahá'u'lláh revealed after the Kitab-i-Aqdas*, p. 174.

Chapter 3: The Dynamics of Growth on the Personal Path to Purpose

1. Bahá'u'lláh, *The Seven Valleys and the Four Valleys*, pp. 13-15.

2. Bahá'u'lláh, "The Glory of God" (1817-1892), born Mirza Husayn-'Alí, is the Prophet-Founder of the Bahá'í Faith. Bahá'u'lláh's Writings, which envision the re-gathering of the human family that has been occurring in the 19th, 20th and 21st Centuries as the vanguard of an emerging, spiritually-centered global civilization, are contained in over one-hundred volumes penned during a forty-year period of exile, imprisonment, and persecution from 1853 to 1892.

3. *Bhagavad Gita* (Edwin Arnold tr.), Chapter X, "The Book of Religion by the Heavenly Perfections." See Interfaith Explorer at BahaiResearch.com

4. Romans 1:19.

5. *Qur'an* 12.

6. Bahá'u'lláh, *The Hidden Words*, #29, from the Persian, p. 32.

7. *Upanishads* vol. 2: Svetasvatara-Upanishad 10.

8. Buddha, *The Word* (The Eightfold Path). See Interfaith Explorer at BahaiResearch.com

9. 1 Peter, 4:1-2.

10. Proverbs 19:15.

11. *Qur'an* (Yusuf Ali tr.) Surah 7.

12. 'Abdu'l-Bahá: *Paris Talks*, pp. 50-51.

Chapter 4: The Spiritual Growth Lab of Life Is Calling Us Toward Spiritual Reality

1. Jeremiah 29:12-13.

2. Matthew 7: 7-8.

3. Deuteronomy 8:3.

4. *Sutta Nipatta* 706.

5. Matthew 6:24.

6. *Qur'an* 62:11.

7. 'Abdu'l-Bahá, quoted in *The Divine Art of Living*, pp. 16-18.

8. 'Abdu'l-Bahá, *Foundations of World Unity*, p. 75.

9. *Bhagavad Gita* 4:37.

10. Sifre Deuteronomy 143a.

11. Shantideva, *Guide to the Bodhisattva's Way of Life* 7:22.

12. 2 Corinthians 12:8-10.

13. *Qur'an* 21:35.

14. 'Abdu'l-Bahá, *Paris Talks*, p. 178.

15. *Laws of Manu* 2:239.

16. Proverbs 3:11-12.

17. Bahá'u'lláh, quoted in Shoghi Effendi, *The Advent of Divine Justice*, p. 82.

18. *Katha Upanishad* 2.1.10.

19. John 14:2.

20. *Qur'an* 71:15.

21. Bahá'u'lláh, *Gleanings from the Writings of Bahá'u'lláh*, p. 127.

22. 1 Corinthians 13:9-12.

23. 'Abdu'l-Bahá, *Foundations of World Unity*, p. 63.

24. *Bhagavad Gita* 3.31-32.

25. Psalms 1:1-3.

26. *Qur'an* 14:24-27.

27. Matthew 7:24-27.

28. 'Abdu'l-Bahá, *Foundations of World Unity*, p. 77.

29. 'Abdu'l-Bahá, *The Promulgation of Universal Peace*, p. 297.

Chapter 5: The Spiritual Growth Lab of Life Is Calling Forth Our True Self

1. *Bhagavad Gita* 6.5-6.

2. *Mishnah*, Abot 1:14.

3. *Samyutta Nikaya* 1:62.

4. Philippians 2:12.

5. *Qur'an* 5:105.

6. Bahá'u'lláh, *Tablets of Bahá'u'lláh revealed after the Kitab-i-Aqdas*, p. 34.

7. *World Scripture, A Comparative Anthology of Sacred Texts*, p. 142. *Mundaka Upanishad* 2.2.1-2.

8. Genesis 1:26.

9. World Scripture, A Comparative Anthology of Sacred Texts, p. 141. *Talmud*, Taanit 11b.

10. *World Scripture, A Comparative Anthology of Sacred Texts*, p. 140. *Mahaparinirvana Sutra* 214.

11. John 14:20.

12. 1 Corinthians 3:16-17.

13. *World Scripture, A Comparative Anthology of Sacred Texts*, p. 141. *Qur'an* 15.29.

14. Bahá'u'lláh, *The Hidden Words*, #11, from the Arabic, p. 6.

15. George Townshend, *The Heart of the Gospel*, p. 29.

16. Leviticus 10:1-2.

17. *Dhammapada* 379-80.

18. *Qur'an* 41:46.

19. Bahá'u'lláh, *The Hidden Words*, #72, from the Persian, p. 47.

20. Romans 7:21-24.

21. *World Scripture, A Comparative Anthology of Sacred Texts*, p. 272. *Mahabharata*.

22. *Avesta*, Yasna 30:3.

23. *Maitri Upanishad* 6:34.

24. 'Abdu'l-Bahá, *Foundations of World Unity*, p. 31.

25. Bahá'u'lláh, *Gleanings from the Writings of Bahá'u'lláh*, p. 68.

26. Mark 1:114-120.

27. *World Scripture, A Comparative Anthology of Sacred Texts*, p. 142. *Mundaka Upanishad* 2.2.1-2.

28. Bahá'u'lláh, *Gleanings from the Writings of Bahá'u'lláh*, pp. 267-268.

29. Bahá'u'lláh, *The Seven Valleys and the Four Valleys*, p. 14.

Chapter 6: The Spiritual Growth Lab of Life Is Calling Us to the Guided Condition

1. *Bhagavad Gita* 4:11.

2. *Qur'an* 5:35.

3. Proverbs 3:5-6.

4. John 6:28-29.

5. *Qur'an* 7:56.

6. Bahá'u'lláh, *The Hidden Words*, #59, from the Arabic, p. 17.

7. *Talmud*, Sota 48b.

8. Matthew 6:31-33.

9. *Qur'an* 29:60.

10. Bahá'u'lláh, *The Hidden Words*, #35, from the Persian, p. 34.

11. *Bhagavad Gita* 5:10-11.

12. 'Abdu'l-Bahá, *Selections from the Writings of 'Abdu'l-Bahá*, p. 146.

13. *The Qur'án* (Rodwell tr.) Sura 6:103-Cattle.

14. *Bhagavad Gita* 18:66.

15. *Mishnah*, Abot 3:6.

16. *Mishnah* Abot 2:4.

17. 'Abdu'l-Bahá, "Servant of Glory" (1844-1921), born Abbas Effendi, is the eldest son of Bahá'u'lláh and, at His passing in 1892, was designated in Bahá'u'lláh's will and testament as the Center of Bahá'u'lláh's Covenant with humankind, the perfect exemplar of His teachings and the sole authorized

interpreter of Bahá'u'lláh's writings during the remainder of his lifetime (the period 1892-1921).

18. 'Abdu'l-Bahá, quoted in *'Abdu'l-Bahá in London*, p. 120.

Chapter 7: The Spiritual Growth Lab of Life Is Calling Us Toward Spiritual Growth

1. Bahá'u'lláh, *The Seven Valleys and the Four Valleys*, p. 15.

2. Romans 5:3-5.

3. *Garland Sutra* 10.

4. *Qur'an* 6:165.

5. Bahá'u'lláh, *The Hidden Words*, #49, from the Arabic, p. 15.

6. Bahá'u'lláh, *The Seven Valleys and the Four Valleys*, pp. 14-15.

7. Bahá'u'lláh, *The Seven Valleys and the Four Valleys*, p. 15.

8. *Dhammapada* 116-118.

9. Bahá'u'lláh, *The Hidden Words*, #8, from the Persian, p. 24.

10. Jeremiah 29:12-13.

11. Matthew 7: 7-8.

12. Bahá'u'lláh, *Tablets of Bahá'u'lláh revealed after the Kitab-i-Aqdas*, p. 235.

13. Adapted from William Bridges, *Managing Transitions*, Addison-Wesley.

14. Alan Scheffer is a Principal of Management Associates, Sioux City, Iowa, and co-author, along with Mark Scheffer and Nancy Braun, of the book, *Hanging the Mirror: The Discipline of Reflective Leadership*.

15. Matthew 23:12.

16. Bahá'u'lláh, *The Hidden Words*, #42, from the Arabic, p. 13.

17. Matthew 5:48.

18. 1 Corinthians 3:16.

19. Bahá'u'lláh, *Gleanings from the Writings of Bahá'u'lláh*, p. 287.

Chapter 8: The Spiritual Growth Lab of Life Is Calling Us Toward Collaborative Rather Than Adversarial Human Interactions

1. Bahá'u'lláh, *The Seven Valleys and the Four Valleys*, p. 15.

2. Isaiah 1:18-20.

3. *Qur'án* 42:36. Cited in 'Abdu'l-Bahá, *The Secret of Divine Civilization*, p. 100.

4. Bahá'u'lláh, *Tablets of Bahá'u'lláh revealed after the Kitab-i-Aqdas*, p. 168.

5. Ibid.

6. 'Abdu'l-Bahá, *The Promulgation of Universal Peace*, pp. 72-73.

7. Bahá'u'lláh, quoted in *Consultation: A Compilation*, p. 3.

8. 'Abdu'l-Bahá, *Selections from the Writings of 'Abdu'l-Bahá*, p. 88.

Chapter 9: Putting Our Learning into Action—Living a Purposeful Life

1. Adapted from *The Tao Book and Card Pack* by Timothy Freke, pp. 41-42.

2. Bahá'u'lláh, *Prayers and Meditations by Bahá'u'lláh*, p. 257.

3. *Yajur Veda* 36:20.

4. *Qur'an* 2:153-157.

5. 'Abdu'l-Bahá, *Paris Talks*, pp. 50-51.

6. Ibid.

7. Robert Bly, *Iron John*, p. 224.

8. *World Scripture, A Comparative Anthology of Sacred Texts*, p. 691. *Hadith of Ibn Majah.*

9. Bahá'u'lláh, *The Hidden Words*, #51, from the Arabic, p. 15.

10. 'Abdu'l-Bahá, *Selections from the Writings of 'Abdu'l-Bahá*, p. 239.

11. Proverbs *4:23.*

12. 'Abdu'l-Bahá, *Foundations of World Unity*, p. 110.

13. *Qur'an* 28:5.

14. Matthew 5:5.

15. Matthew 7:7-8.

16. Patty McConnell, *A Workbook for Healing*, p. 22.

17. *Mishnah*, Abot 4:21.

18. Matthew 6:19-21.

19. *Qur'an* 18:46.

20. Bahá'u'lláh, *Gleanings from the Writings of Bahá'u'lláh*, p. 328.

21. 'Abdu'l-Bahá, *Foundations of World Unity*, p. 78.

22. Bahá'u'lláh, *The Hidden Words*, #18, from the Arabic, p. 8.

23. 'Abdu'l-Bahá, *Selections from the Writings of 'Abdu'l-Bahá*, p. 245.

24. Bahá'u'lláh, *Gleanings from the Writings of Bahá'u'lláh*, p. 271.

25. Mark Twain, *Pudd'nhead Wilson*, p. 15.

26. Bahá'u'lláh, *The Hidden Words*, #17, from the Arabic, p. 8.

27. Bahá'u'lláh, *The Hidden Words*, #15, from the Arabic, p. 7.

28. *Chandogya Upanishad* 7:23.

29. Psalms 16:11.

30. Romans 14:17.

31. *Qur'an* 32:17.

32. 'Abdu'l-Bahá, *Tablets of 'Abdu'l-Bahá*, v3, p. 557.

33. 'Abdu'l-Bahá, *Paris Talks*, p. 108.

34. Bahá'u'lláh, *The Seven Valleys and the Four Valleys*, p. 14.

35. Bahá'u'lláh, *Gleanings from the Writings of Bahá'u'lláh*, p. 129.

36. Psalms 10.1-4.

37. Romans 1.19-20.

38. *Qur'an* 41.53.

39. Bahá'u'lláh, *The Hidden Words*, #29, from the Persian, p. 32.

40. Cited in Bahá'u'lláh, *The Book of Certitude*, p. 67. See also Thomas Patrick Hughes, *The Dictionary of Islam*, p. 145.

41. Bahá'u'lláh, *The Book of Certitude*, p. 167.

42. Jalāl ad-Dīn Muhammad Rūmī, (1207-1273), "Not Always On," 1 April 2004, 29 July 2011 http://www.elise.com/we-blog/archives/000312guest_house_-_rumi.php.

43. Bahá'u'lláh, *The Hidden Words*, #18, from the Arabic, p. 8.

44. Hebrews 13:2.

45. Bahá'u'lláh, *The Proclamation of Bahá'u'lláh*, p. 116.

46. Portia Nelson, *There's a Hole in My Sidewalk: The Romance of Self Discovery*.

47. Romans, 12:3.

48. 'Abdu'l-Bahá, *The Promulgation of Universal Peace*, Part 2, p. 244.

49. *Qur'an* 4:28.

50. Bahá'u'lláh, quoted in *Bahá'í Prayers*, p. 211-212.

51. Bahá'u'lláh, *The Hidden Words*, #56, from the Arabic, p. 16-17.

52. *Qur'an* 12.64.

53. *Rig Veda* 7:100:4.

54. *Avesta*, Yasna 34:15.

55. Hosea 6:1-2.

56. *Srimad Bhagavatam* 11:2.

57. 2 Timothy 2:13.

58. Bahá'u'lláh, quoted in *Bahá'í Prayers*, p. 194.

59. *Mahabharata*, Shanti Parva 329.

60. *Dhammapada* 171.

61. Romans 12:2.

62. *Forty Hadith of an-Nawawi* 31.

63. Bahá'u'lláh, *Gleanings from the Writings of Bahá'u'lláh*, p. 276.

64. Bahá'u'lláh, *Tablets of Bahá'u'lláh revealed after the Kitab-i-Aqdas*, p. 17.

65. 'Abdu'l-Bahá, *Selections from the Writings of 'Abdu'l-Bahá*, p. 120.

66. Malachi 3:3.

67. 1 Corinthians 10:13.

68. *Qur'an* 65:7.

69. Adib Taherzadeh, *The Revelation of Bahá'u'lláh*, Vol. 1, pp. 269-270.

70. Bahá'u'lláh, *Gleanings from the Writings of Bahá'u'lláh*, p. 129.

71. *Qur'an* (Yusuf Ali tr.) 39:10.

72. Bahá'u'lláh, *The Hidden Words*, #9, from the Arabic, p. 5.

73. *World Scripture, A Comparative Anthology of Sacred Texts*, p. 684. *Basavanna*, Vacana 247.

74. *Mishnah*, Abot 1:2.

75. *World Scripture, A Comparative Anthology of Sacred Texts*, p. 686. *Perfection of Wisdom in Eight Thousand Lines* 321-22.

76. 1Timothy 5:1-2.

77. *World Scripture, A Comparative Anthology of Sacred Texts,* p. 94. *Hadith of Baihaqi.*

78. Bahá'u'lláh, *Tablets of Bahá'u'lláh revealed after the Kitab-i-Aqdas,* p. 163.

79. *Brihadaranyaka Upanishad* 5:2.2: The Voice of Thunder.

80. *Talmud,* Taanit 11a.

81. Galatians 6:2.

82. *World Scripture, A Comparative Anthology of Sacred Texts,* p. 688. *Hadith of Bukhari.*

83. Psalms 92:14-15.

84. Ephesians 5:9.

85. *Qur'an* (Pickthall tr): 6:99 - The Cattle.

86. Bahá'u'lláh, *Epistle to the Son of the Wolf,* p. 19.

87. *Bhagavad Gita* 2:22-25.

88. Ecclesiastes 12:7.

89. 2 Corinthians 4:16-18.

90. *Qur'an* 41:39.

91. Bahá'u'lláh, *Gleanings from the Writings of Bahá'u'lláh,* p. 161.

92. Bahá'u'lláh, *The Seven Valleys and the Four Valleys,* p. 6.